# BLAGGERS

# BLAGGERS

## ADVENTURES INSIDE THE SUN-KISSED BUT MURKY WORLD OF HOLIDAY TIMESHARE

## BARRY LEY

MAINSTREAM
PUBLISHING

EDINBURGH AND LONDON

First published in Great Britain in 2001 by
MAINSTREAM PUBLISHING COMPANY (EDINBURGH) LTD
7 Albany Street
Edinburgh EH1 3UG

ISBN 1 84018 438 8

A catalogue record for this book is available from the British Library

Typeset in Van Dijck and Khaki
Printed and bound in Great Britain by Cox and Wyman Ltd

# CONTENTS

# PROLOGUE

The meeting was in Manelli's office. Plush and extravagant, it was set overlooking his luxurious Canary island timeshare development. A king needs to survey his kingdom after all.

Jock met us at the entrance to the Mayfair Club and, wordlessly eyeing up the sharp lightweight suits we had chosen to wear, ushered us up to the big man's throne room.

As we waited we tried to mooch around in a suitably gangster-like manner. Luckily we had seen all the films, so we knew how to behave when meeting the Capo. Blissfully oblivious to how ridiculous we looked, we sat there poker-faced, and waited.

After about fifteen minutes, in walked Marlon Brando. Not the real one, obviously, but an impressive enough imitation to our inexperienced eyes. The suit, the hair, the mannerisms. They all screamed Cosa Nostra. Looking back on it now, I am inclined to believe that he was, in fact, just a run-of-the-mill Italian businessman who had invested in timeshare. But we could not have been more impressed.

'So boys,' he rasped, 'a drink?'

'Whisky, straight!' I growled, while Tom asked politely if he could have a Ribena.

His secretary scampered smirking from the room and Manelli gestured to the large leather chaise-longue by the French windows. We sat. He appeared to meditate upon his opening words. As we waited, his secretary came back in.

'Here are your drinks,' she grinned, handing them over. 'I

couldn't find any whisky so I got you a Ribena too.'

As we sipped, Manelli fixed us with his steely gaze.

'Balls!' he declared. 'I need people with balls in my organisation. Tell me. Do you have cojones? Do you have what it takes to be on my team?'

'Would we be here otherwise, Mr Manelli?' said Tom smoothly, with a slight Italian accent.

I said nothing but regarded him coolly.

'Jock has been telling me good things about you two,' he continued. 'He tells me that you did a good job with my photo team and that you've been getting results. I hear you have been having problems with the two gorillas from Oasis, huh?'

Presumably he meant Pete and Alex, our psychopathic previous employers. We nodded expectantly.

'Worry no more. Nobody fucks with my operation. I have sent for those clowns. They'll be here soon and when they get here I, Manelli, will put the fear of God into them. After this meeting they won't dare to speak to you again. You will sit there and say nothing. Observe the power of Manelli!'

There did not seem to be any reply to this, so we sat in silence. We were a little uneasy about the thought of Pete and Alex being dealt with in front of us but maybe it was for the best. They could hardly fail to be intimidated by such an awesome sounding Goodfella as Manelli. After they had been put back firmly in their place, they would know that from that moment on Tom and I would be untouchable. They would have to keep out of our way and it would be a lesson in humility for them. We settled back on the chaise-longue and waited to savour the moment that they arrived.

We didn't have long to wait. Noise from the outer office told us that Pete and Alex had turned up. Manelli stood. He walked over to a large painting on the wall. He stood facing it, away from the doorway. His manicured hands were clasped behind his back. He was obviously going to ignore the big fellas when they came in, for dramatic effect. Cool as a cucumber, he studied a particularly fascinating part of his picture without so much as glancing round when they entered. Pete and Alex, however, weren't interested in playing games. They marched over as one menacing force and without a word proceeded to beat him to a pulp.

'Wha . . ?' began Manelli. He was in a lot of pain and clearly finding it difficult to believe what was happening to him.

'We . . . are . . . not . . . pizzas!' explained Pete, emphasising every word with a vicious blow to Manelli's nose. 'You . . . do . . . not . . . send . . . out . . . for . . . us!'

Tom and I froze in our seats. Everything was going horribly wrong. The blood drained from our faces and our jaws hung slackly open. Time slowed down as Pete and Alex finished 'having a word' with Manelli, their attention turned towards us. Our mutual gaze locked across the Italian's prostrate form and I could see in Pete's eyes that he wasn't at all happy.

Consumed by rage might have been a better way of putting it. Either way I was getting out of there. I snapped out of my daze before Tom.

'Run for it!' I screamed over my shoulder as I bolted for the doorway. Tom did not need telling twice. Linford Christie wouldn't have caught us as we pelted through the sales area of the Mayfair Club. We pulled tables and chairs over in our wake to try and slow them down. All the while they sounded as though they were within grabbing distance.

Don't ask me how but we made it to the car before they caught us. We dived in and locked the doors. Just to be on the safe side, I knocked Alex's motorbike over with the car before we drove off.

There was no need to discuss anything when we got back to the apartment. We threw all our stuff into bags in about a minute and a half, after which we shrieked off to the airport.

'Holland or England?' gasped Tom.

'England!' I panted back.

There was a flight to Manchester one hour later and we were on it. Jetting away from trouble and towards . . . well, we didn't really know what we were jetting towards. We only knew that for the time being we would be safe in England.

# 1

# A SHADY BUSINESS?

Well no, not really. Oh, I know what you're thinking: timeshare rip-off merchants, the annoying little pests that rank up there second only to cockroaches on your list of holiday pests. They dog you every time you step outside of your hotel and they won't take no for an answer. Scratch cards and invitations, free taxis and bribes of booze and fags. You're just not interested, right? If you wanted to buy a timeshare you would bloody well have approached them already!

I can understand and sympathise that it must be a right royal pain from the point of view of someone who has worked hard all year just to pay for a couple of weeks' quiet holiday. If you're the kind of person who gets vexed easily, I'm sure it must drive you to distraction.

There is a solution. The next time you see a tout standing on some hot Spanish corner, give them a smile. We're only human after all and are always grateful to be treated as such. You don't have to visit the timeshare but you'll soon find that you've made a new friend who knows where the best restaurants and bars are. We're generally a better source of information than your average holiday rep about the place where you're staying as we don't have to recommend dubious excursions and a dodgy nightlife just because the head rep gets a kickback from them. As I said, you don't have to visit the timeshare complex itself, but if you do get friendly with a tout you should be able to negotiate suitable recompense. A couple of hundred fags and a bottle of whisky is not too bad for an hour of your time after all, and it puts a few quid in the tout's pocket.

Ah but it's not just them, is it? It's the ones inside the complex when you get there. The ones with the fins on their backs. The real sharks who lick their lips in quivering anticipation at the mere thought of an opportunity to wrench the life savings from some poor old dear who walks too close to the complex. The truth is that there are people like that but they genuinely make up a tiny percentage. The Spanish authorities came down hard on all the cowboy companies in the late '90s and these days take a very dim view of people messing with their lucrative tourist trade. If you go to one of the modern presentations while on your next holiday the chances are that you will actually have an enjoyable morning. And whether you sign up or not, you'll have found out what all the fuss is about.

Last year 1.25 million Brits had timeshare holidays and that number is increasing every year. These days even the large holiday companies have stopped putting us down and, having failed to beat us, have finally decided to join us: Airtours, Thomsons and First Choice are all involved in promoting their own 'Holiday Ownership' complexes in the Canary and Balearic Islands – very successfully too I might add!

But my book is not set in the sanitised environment of timeshare in the early twenty-first century. When I started in the business it was something akin to the lawless Wild West. Huge fearsome criminals ran their empires with ruthless abandon and to make money you had to be both fast and sharp. The only industry guidelines worth noting were to earn money in any way possible and spend it equally quickly on hard living. Keeping your wits about you at all times was a prerequisite. It was fast and loose and not everyone came out unscathed. But oh, the quality of life!

As one of the ones who made it through this sub-tropical chaos, I will say this – I'd do it all again!

# 2

# TENERIFE

At ten o'clock in the morning the sun's rays were already searing through the bright, blue sky. I was in Playa de Las Americas in the south of Tenerife, nervously making my way to my first 'timeshare touts' training session.

The events of the last few weeks had propelled me towards this moment in much the same way as the Niagara Falls propels those people who wake up one morning and decide to give barrel-sailing a try.

It had all started when my best friend's sister, Joanne, got herself recruited from some dodgy seminar in Manchester and found herself in Tenerife touting for a timeshare company a month later. She soon discovered that there was a one hundred pound bonus for tricking friends and loved ones into becoming part of the timeshare team and so, bingo, there I was. Looking into her big blue eyes it had all made sense. I was going to be a millionaire before I was thirty. And if people got hurt along the way, that was their look out. If they couldn't stand the heat, they could get out of my kitchen! Anyway with fifty quid in Spanish money I had set off to take on the world. I spent over half of this on the first night. I had been met at the airport by the company driver and taken to the free accommodation provided for new touts. From there I had made a bee-line for the famous Veronica's Strip. Plenty of my soon-to-be-colleagues were there to welcome me. They were overflowing with hints and tips to make my new job easier (whilst making sure I bought all the drinks). Fortunately, Joanne was there and it was reassuring to see a friendly face. This was to be the first of many drunken nights among the bars and clubs at the Veronica's. A word of warning, if you're over forty, do not go! You'll only think that you somehow took a wrong turn and ended up in Hell. For us normal people though, it was a wonderful place.

The date was June in 1988 and I was eighteen years old. All the new recruits, fourteen of us in total, were trying to walk off our hangovers in the 200 yards between our company housing and the marketing office. No matter how much of a beating I had given my liver the previous night, it was hard not to be optimistic. I crossed the beautiful palm-lined street and headed into the stunning holiday haven of the Oasis Beach Club timeshare. The office was a converted chalet in which my fellow would-be touts and I dutifully took seats in front of the lecture screen. I had never seen so many cut-throats, vagabonds and ex-double-glazing sales people in one room. I surreptitiously tightened my grip on the money in my pocket as we got down to business. The first thing we learned was that we weren't touts we were 'OPCs'. OPC stands for On-sight Personal Contact. As I found out more about what the job entailed, however, I began to suspect that the average tourist might find Over Persistent Cunt closer to the mark. Basically the job of an OPC is to stalk helpless holidaymakers and talk them into looking round timeshare resorts. In those days the OPC got fifteen pounds just for persuading a couple to go and see the timeshare, more if they bought one. In training we were taught our guidelines: we weren't allowed to directly lie; we were, however, allowed to exaggerate. And we did. We exaggerated out of our arses. Couples were naturally more disposed to spending the day on the beach than with some oily little leech of a timeshare salesman. So we were taught to exaggerate along the lines that we wanted to take them to a new beach, with free drinks and watersports, and Elvis would be playing there, and so on.

'Are you sure this isn't timeshare?' they would ask us.

'Of course I'm sure!' we would protest as we ushered them into a taxi.

Their fare would be paid to and from Oasis and they would even receive a small free gift. If you were lucky, there was a good chance that the couple would waste an entire day in the place.

After three days of intensive training and role-play, the manager told us we were ready. We were instructed to go to the morning meeting at nine o'clock the next day. This was the daily motivation session before work and it was performed by the big fellas: two huge charismatic body-builders from mean streets of Darlington called Pete and Alex. Hard men, they ran Oasis with a collective iron fist. Alex looked like a blond copy of the Terminator, with his severe flat-top hairstyle and nineteen stone, 6ft 3in. physique. Pete was an inch shorter and looked like a ferocious pumped-up version of Brian Ferry. At twenty-eight he was a year older than Alex. They were our marketing managers. They did not look like marketing managers. They looked instead like they were paid to ride around all day on big motorbikes, showing off their muscles and attracting the birds, principally because, besides intimidating the workforce, that's all they seemed to do.

Before my first meeting, I had been racking my brains and came up with what I thought was a good strategy for OPCing – a competitive edge, if you will. I had observed that everyone wore shorts and t-shirts for work. After much contemplation on the subject, I came up with this: I would make myself stand out from the crowd by dressing smartly. At this point of my life 'smart' meant chino shorts, with shirt and tie and brown suede shoes. The plan was that couples would notice me among the rest of the OPCs. The only slight worry I had was about turning up to the morning meeting dressed so differently to everybody else. So as not to attract too much derision I was hoping to slip in before the others and hide quietly at the back.

So there I was, nice and early outside the marketing office door waiting for the meeting. Nine o'clock came and went without a single person turning up. I was just starting to wonder why everyone else was so late when it occurred to me that I was at the wrong office.

Oh shit! I thought, as I sprinted round to where the meeting was actually taking place.

Out of breath I burst into the room. Unluckily for me, I hadn't realised quite how crowded it would be. One hundred and twenty OPCs were all crammed into the room sitting, sagely contemplating the day's touting ahead, when in I flew. Tripping over the tightly packed group of people by the door, I sailed through the air, tie flapping gracefully over my shoulder, to land on some girls in the centre of the office. The fact that they were enjoying a takeaway breakfast of bacon sandwiches and orange juice didn't help matters much.

'Watch where you're going, you prick!' they muttered aggressively.

As I shakily managed to extricate myself from the tangle of bronzed limbs, I glanced nervously around the sea of shocked faces.

It was only then that the full effect of my 'Dress for Success' strategy achieved it's terrible impact.

'Jesus!' said someone.

'A shirt and tie?' said someone else.

'But we're in Tenerife!' declared a third. 'What a twat!'

At this point Pete, the more fearsome of our two marketing managers, entered the room from the side office ready to start the meeting. I prayed for him to get on with it and thus shift the focus of attention away from my shenanigans. It wasn't to be. He glanced proudly round at his professional-looking pack of OPCs as he confidently strode towards his desk at the front. Then he noticed me. He stopped in his tracks. His jaw dropped as he looked me up and down. For a few seconds we stood there, sizing each other up. The contrast between his powerful, tanned chest and my orange juice-soaked shirt was painfully apparent. Mocking laughter from the OPCs echoed round the room.

'Yes, well, sit down,' said Pete, clearing his throat.

Collecting himself with a brisk shake of his head, he continued to his desk. I brushed a piece of bacon from my shirt collar and sat down miserably among the crowd. I just wanted to get out of there so I could hide for the rest of the day and lick my wounds. I looked at the floor and tried to let the meeting pass me by as I concentrated on being invisible.

Suddenly a warning bell in my brain jolted me back to attention. Fresh horror struck me as I tuned back in to what Pete was saying. Apparently, whenever a group of new OPCs joined the existing team, there was an initiation ceremony in the form of a game played called 'Desert Island'. Pete was happily booming that he needed a volunteer from us new boys to, 'come to the front and stand on this desk facing everybody!'.

Not me, not me, not me, I silently intoned, concentrating on the floor between my legs.

'What about the twat with the tie?' piped up some bastard at the back.

'Yes, you. Twat with the tie. Up you come!' beamed Pete.

I trudged wretchedly up to the front, wiped the drop of orange juice from the end of my nose and climbed onto the desk. With monumental effort I stood and turned to face the OPCs. All I could hope for was a quick death. Or at least that the approaching ordeal wouldn't last too long.

Come on then, let's get it over with, I was thinking as I grinned weakly at the hostile crowd.

Just then the phone rang in the other office.

'OK everyone, stay where you are, I'll be right back,' said Pete as he went to answer it.

Stay where we are? Stay where we fucking are? I might as well have been holding a sign saying 'Taunt Me!' for the next ten minutes while Pete chattered away oblivious on the phone. I shuffled my feet, stared out of the window and studiously ignored the snide remarks until he came back in.

Desert Island consisted of Pete telling a story about me getting shipwrecked on an ocean voyage. During the story there would be pauses while he waited for me to provide the appropriate sound effect. For example, he would say, 'The wind blew waves over the side of the boat,' then pause, which was my cue to go, 'Woosh! Woosh!' with as much gusto as I could manage.

At the end of the story it turned out that I was floating on a piece of driftwood big enough for only one other person. Pete then informed me that I had to choose who, out of all the female OPCs,

I was going to save to keep as a sex slave on my desert island. He looked at me expectantly.

'Choose one then!' he demanded.

As I looked round the room it occurred to me that I would rather let go of my driftwood and drown than subject myself to the humiliation of the impending rejection. Nevertheless, steeling myself against her reaction, I pointed to a pretty girl at the back.

'Her there then!' I blurted. 'Can I go now?'

The meeting did eventually end, and I survived of course, but I still maintain that it was bad luck picking the only transvestite in the room.

It was a very broad cross-section of society, as well as many different nationalities who made up the trabajadores extranjeros or immigrant workforce. Princess Caroline's cousin, for example, was working alongside bank robbers from South London. I met drug dealers and poets. I drank with thieves and thespians. Everyone had a reason not to want to be back in their home country and everyone had their own story. It made for interesting times. In the beginning those of us who were skint used to have parties at our company accommodation. Oasis Beach Club used to rent out one side of a nearby hotel so that us new OPCs wouldn't have to worry about having a roof over our heads while we were learning the job. Sometimes I think that those times, when we were all potless, were the best of all. We used to cook pasta and get hammered on cheap local wine by the pool, in the balmy Spanish evenings. And of course there was the sex. It was the first time in my life that I had slept with any foreign girls, and I thought myself rather cosmopolitan and smug.

Working in timeshare was where the money was made. The other jobs were bar work or PRing. A 'PR' is a tout who stands outside a bar on the strip. The job of a PR is to talk tourists into going for a drink in the bar that he or she works for, and so earn their commission. Bar work and PRing were the easy options. Very little money but free drinks all night and more tourists to bonk than you could shake a stick at. This combined with having every daytime relaxing by the beach (or snoring the day away in their stinking pits) meant that, all in all, these two jobs provided regular money and a good lifestyle for most of the younger travellers.

Timeshare was (and still is) a commission only business. If you don't perform, you don't get paid, but the rewards are sky high for those people prepared to put in the time. During training I was dreaming about how I was going to spend all the money I was going to earn. It all sounded so easy. As long I said the right things, didn't let the tourists get me down and came up with all the right answers at the right times, I was going to score big-time.

Except, of course, that at first I didn't. I had assumed that by working near the best OPCs and by copying their style and patter, I would do as well as them – better in fact, when you factored in my youthful enthusiasm and drive.

I was working the beachfront one day with Ben Hinks – a thin, extremely streetwise character from Liverpool with a blond ponytail and freckles. He was in his late twenties and one of Oasis' superstar OPCs. With his flash manner and his ability to talk complete strangers into just about anything, he was one of my heroes.

'Watch me, kiddo, and you'll be all right,' he instructed generously as he surveyed the oncoming crowd.

I watched and listened. He sidled slyly up to a couple and fell in step.

'All right dere folks, 'ows it goin'?' he inquired of them.

They looked around at him, wondering where he'd come from.

'Er, OK thanks,' they ventured.

'Good, good. Here's your promotion card,' he said, pushing one of his tickets dismissively, even absently, towards them.

They hesitated, weighing up the situation. Taking the ticket seemed to be their easiest escape route.

'Right, well, see you then,' they said, making as if to continue on their way. Ben appeared to have lost interest in them, when suddenly he clapped his hand to his head in realisation.

'Sorry mate, I've only gone and forgotten to put my name on that ticket!'

And in one lightning move he was standing in front of them. His skinny little frame was somehow blocking their entire path as he laboriously copied his name onto the card. The couple's body language was screaming out their desire to be rid of him. Ben refused to notice.

'So, how's your holiday going?' he asked as he painstakingly wrestled with the letter 'e'.

'Look pal,' began the husband, who had clearly decided that it was time to assert himself.

Ben ignored him completely.

'Bet you've had a few good nights on the beer, haven't you?' he winked conspiratorially as he turned to focus his charm on the wife. 'Has he love? Has he been showing you up?'

Ben nudged her, cheeky grin perfectly in place, and her defences cracked.

''As 'e 'eckers like, it's bin me what's bin showing 'im up!' she cackled. 'Come on then, tell us what you're promoting.'

Hubby sized up the situation. His obviously domineering wife seemed to have, for some reason, taken a shine to the little weasel. His least embarrassing option now was to pretend that he had too.

'Yeah, come on, tell us,' he said, resignedly settling into his role.

Ben smoothly rattled off his spiel like the master he was. Within five minutes he was stopping a taxi to take them to Oasis.

'See you John! See you Doris! And don't you forget what a good lad I've been when you see my boss up there!' he enthused sickeningly.

They all said their hearty goodbyes. As the taxi sped off towards the timeshare complex, John and Doris shouted promises to buy Ben a drink later. Ben fawned after them until they had disappeared round the corner. Then he turned back towards me and the smarminess vanished from his face completely like the early-morning dew. His usual streetwise demeanour instantly clicked back into place.

'That's how you do it old son. Easy, isn't it? Come on, it's your turn.'

He's right, that's bloody easy, I thought. Not wishing to waste a further second I bounded over to an approaching couple, confidently extending a ticket.

'Hi there! Enjoying your holiday?' I beamed, charm oozing from every pore.

'Fuck off, son.'

Aha, I thought, not the reaction I was hoping for. Still, I had been trained to deal with this. My smile assured them that I hadn't been offended in the least.

'It's OK, I'm only promoting . . .'

'Look, are you going to fuck off?'

No problem, I told myself. Do not be put off. They are bound to be a bit sceptical at first. I've just got to show them what a pleasant, harmless young fellow I really am. I tried again.

'You see, my name's Barry and I've just started working for . . .'

'Because if you don't fuck off, I'm going to smash your face in!'

Enough was enough. He was obviously not going to take any of my shit! I sat down on the wall, perplexed. What had I done wrong? Why on earth would any couple prefer an annoying, persistent little toerag like Ben, when they could do a favour for an amiable, genuine person like myself? I couldn't understand it. Whatever the reason, over the next two weeks I found that my first attempt at a pitch was to set the tone for the ones that followed. I was thoroughly enjoying the island, being away from home and living in the sun. The beaches, nightlife and people were great. I was making loads of new and interesting friends. The one fly in the sangria was that I didn't seem to be able to do the job. I began to believe that it was beyond my capabilities. No matter how enthusiastic and determined I was, the rejections came fast and furious. After this initial fortnight of failing to get to grips with OPCing it was with my head hanging in utter dejection that I went to see Pete. My resignation speech prepared, I took a deep breath and knocked on his office door. I readied myself for the 'Never mind at least you tried' platitudes as I stepped inside.

'Ah, Tie Boy!' said Pete looking up from his game of backgammon. 'How can I help you?'

I poured out my pitiful tale of hardship. I described the battle against insurmountable odds and poverty that I had undertaken in my bid to serve him well. I only had about one pound fifty left from my stake money and I explained that, with such little funding, I had decided to call it a day.

'Yes, yes, yes,' said Pete disinterestedly, as he began oiling down his muscles. 'Just pop your accommodation keys in the losers tray over there, and close the door on your way out.'

Just a minute, I thought, that's not the reaction I was after! I sprang to my own defence.

'Look, I've tried my hardest. I've got a quid and a half left in my pocket. What do you want me to do?' I whined pathetically. Pete levelled me with his gaze.

'Barry, if you want something bad enough nothing will get in your way. There are no excuses for giving up. Do you want to be a good OPC?' he asked.

I nodded miserably, wondering what more I could possibly do. His expression softened ever so slightly.

'Look, I've seen you working. You're too nice to the couples. They're walking all over you. Think about yourself from now on. Start lying, cheating and conning people more and you'll be just fine.'

With that, he grabbed his motorbike keys, baseball cap and shades, and set off to chat up some girls.

Small encouragement you might think, but it was enough. My determination renewed, I threw away my return ticket. I marched to the supermarket and spent my remaining money on cheap Spanish bread and drinking water.

Lying, cheating and conning people, eh? I got stuck right in. My scruples went out of the window. From that point on no lie was too devious, no falsehood too blatant. I would say whatever it took to trick the couple in front of me into visiting our timeshare. My tenacity paid off. The very next week I had 11 ups (an 'up' was what we called a couple that we had taken to the club). The week after, I had 21. The week after that I had 28 ups and 7 deals (a deal is when an up actually buys a timeshare during their visit and the OPC gets a bonus of around one hundred pounds). Soon I was ranking alongside the best OPCs, but it wasn't enough. I'd been hearing rumours of an elite band of touts who worked for our company during the night. A sleeker, more sophisticated group who got a huge number of ups, dressed smartly for work and were given company cars. They were called 'the photo team'.

The photo team was a marketing strategy of Pete's. You see, when an OPC brings an up to the club, that's the end of his or her involvement in the process. For the couple it is just beginning. An OPC has the option of whether or not to accompany the up in the taxi. Either way, when the couple arrive at the club they are then met by a receptionist who takes responsibility for them and pays off the taxi. From there they are taken into reception and made to feel at ease while being 'qualified' (asked their date of birth, whether or not they are home owners etc – this is done to make sure that they fit into the correct demograph of a likely candidate for timeshare ownership). Once the couple have qualified and agreed to the presentation, the receptionist hands them over to a salesperson who then attempts to pressurise them into signing on the dotted line before they leave. These salespeople have fixed hours. At Oasis their working day was from ten o'clock in the morning until five o'clock in the afternoon. We could only bring couples to the resort while the salespeople were working, so, after five o'clock, we effectively couldn't work, meaning that couples were safe to walk the streets. Pete had never been happy about this. It just didn't seem right to him that tourists should be free to wander round doing whatever they wanted to, without making him any money. Having given the problem some serious consideration he had come up with a solution: a special group of particularly persistent and shameless OPCs was selected to work in the bars and restaurants of an evening. Pete's theory was that once a couple was actually sitting down eating a meal or having a drink, it would be harder for them to ignore or to escape from an OPC who attempted to pitch them.

Now, you're most likely thinking that's just taking the piss and, well, you'd probably be right. It wasn't merely a case of blatantly walking up to your potential victims and steaming right in with the hard sell though, it was done in carefully planned stages. The first thing the photo team would do upon entering a chosen bar would be to go round the tables and take a free photo of every couple in the place (hence the name), explaining that it was obligation free and that the pictures could be collected from the bar the following night. This way they could get chatting to the couples and offer them drinks vouchers as bribes to book in for a visit to Oasis Beach Club the next morning.

The photo OPCs worked in teams of two. Each team had a company camera, a group of bars and the use of a Fiat Panda, which could be upgraded at the OPC's own expense. They made bookings at night which they picked up and drove to Oasis the next morning. Altogether preferable to sweating and burning all day in the sub-tropical sun.

The problem was, it was very hard to get on to the photo team. Any new OPC who asked Pete got turned down flat. It was pointless asking my street captain, Melon Man, for help because he was getting paid an override on my ups (he got about ten pounds every time I got a couple up to Oasis) and wanted to keep me on his team. What could I do? I was anxious to become a photo OPC so I had to come up with a cunning plan. Now, I new that each photo team had one day off per week, like us street OPCs. Also, street OPCs were allowed to go to the night-time photo meeting to check the day's numbers (results of the day's work e.g., how many couples were 'paid on' and how many were not Qualified or NQ'd).

Normally, I would get my numbers at the morning meeting the next day but I started turning up at the night meetings because I had an ulterior motive. I would check my numbers while noting which of the photo OPCs wasn't working that night. Then I would surreptitiously check the bar list on the wall to see which bars and restaurants they normally covered. I would then sneak round these bars and work them myself. My plan worked brilliantly until people began to suspect. It ruffled their feathers that I was working on their patch.

Dark mutterings began to echo round the photo meetings to the effect that the description given by couples of the phantom photo

OPC was suspiciously close to that of me. Eventually, someone voiced their feelings to Pete. I was sitting quietly in the corner of the meeting one night, camera hidden in my trousers, when I heard him bellowing my name from the inner office. Sensing trouble, I was trying to sneak out of the room when he stuck his head round the door and summoned me in directly for a private chat.

'You're a sneaky little bastard!' he told me after I had closed the door.

'Whaddya mean?' I retorted self-righteously.

'Why have you got a camera in your pants?' he asked pointedly.

'Er, taking a photo of my knob,' I tried.

'No, you're sneaking round people's bars on their nights off!' he said firmly.

I could see carefully concealed amusement in his eyes. He was obviously proud of the monster he had created.

'Barry, you know how I like to encourage dishonesty and believe me I'm very pleased with how far you've come, but . . .' (He frowned slightly as he decided on how best to express himself.) '. . . I can't have you upsetting all my other workers. Look, wait outside and I'll deal with you after the meeting.'

I skulked back outside. Punishment depended on the seriousness of the offence. It varied. You could get off with a fine for a minor transgression like excessive lying at work (to the extent that the company lost business). At the other end of the scale, however, things could get nasty. If you really upset Pete and Alex you would simply get a right good kicking. This was – I should add – only internal punishment from the company. Everyone in timeshare was working illegally, so we had to be constantly alert for the police when we were working the street. I have been deported, beaten up, even driven ten miles into the mountains in the back of a police car where I was dumped, minus my shoes, meaning that I had to walk barefoot all the way back to town. By the time I turned up at my complex, exhausted and with my feet cut to ribbons, my shoes were waiting for me in reception. The police, probably falling over themselves with laughter, had dropped them off to wind me up.

However, I've also scammed the police on several occasions.

Every time I've been deported, I've merely bought a ticket back to Blighty for one of my friends who wanted to go home – as long as he was roughly the same age, and had similar coloured hair, it was no problem to swap passports and send them back to Britain in my place. I could continue working with the other guy's passport until we exchanged them back by post.

But I digress. Let us return to the scene of my younger self sitting gloomily at the back of the photo meeting trying to anticipate what particular punishment I would receive.

As it happened luck was on my side. One of the photo OPCs had committed a serious offence that day. Jennifer, who was one of the few OPCs who worked on her own, had taken a backhander from a rival company. She had brought some of our customers to them and Pete had found out. During the meeting he sacked her on the spot and, as she was walking out in disgrace, he took her car keys and camera from her and handed them to me. He then announced that as of now, I was promoted to the photo team and would be taking over Jennifer's bars, as a reward for having a good attitude.

From that point on there was no stopping me. As a legitimate member of the photo team I was earning five hundred pounds a week tax free. Within a week or so I was teamed up with Joanne, my friend from England, and we were earning over twelve hundred pounds a week between us. And spending it. We had upgraded our car to two convertible Golf GTIs. I was living in a four-star hotel called La Pinta, sharing with a gang of French lads and lasses who were also doing well. We were getting all our meals sent up by room service, we only had to put our laundry in the chute and it would be back in our room the next day, washed, dried and ironed. Six hundred quid a week is still quite a lot of money now, back in 1988 it was a bloody fortune.

There was a lot of casual sex going on in that apartment. Tourists mainly, as they were more impressed with us than our co-workers were. My flatmates were all older than me, more experienced and French. I therefore had the opportunity to observe skilled practitioners, of both sexes, in the art of getting members of the opposite sex into bed. I took full advantage of their generosity in teaching their young English protégé. I wasn't a bad-looking lad. At 5ft 8in.with a slim frame and floppy dark blond hair cut in the bobbed style that was cool at the time, I could hold my own with any of them. Under the guidance of my French companions I soon became a moderately accomplished blagger. Blagger is a common expression among timeshare and bar touts. It comes from the verb 'to blag' meaning to lie, to trick someone into doing something or to get someone into bed.

Anyway, life was all going rather well, except that I wasn't saving any money from my wages. Everyone was telling me that I should put some away for harsher times but I didn't, because I knew better. I thought that this good spell would last forever. I was about to learn what seems now to be par for the course in my life: when everything is going right, it goes wrong.

A cloud was beginning to form on the horizon. The cloud's name was Ron. He had been hanging around the fringes of my particular social circle for a while. A pugnacious-looking thug of a man, he was about thirty years old with short dark hair. He was a bit shorter than me but thick set and covered in body hair. He used to turn up with cases of shop-lifted goods and try to sell them at the OPC meetings. He had the demeanour of someone who is always up to no good. A sly attitude that made people constantly on edge when he was around. I didn't really pay much attention to him at first. I was working on the assumption that if I gave him no opportunity to steal from me, he would slope off back to wherever it was that he had come from.

Then one evening, Joanne, my close friend and trusted working partner, turned up to the photo meeting glowing with obvious happiness. I tried to ignore it, but eventually my curiosity got the better of me.

'All right, this has gone far enough,' I complained. 'Tell me why you're so happy.'

'Barry, I'm in love!' she gushed. Plainly she had been waiting for me to ask.

'Who with?' I inquired cautiously, my mind racing through possibilities. This girl did not fall in love easily.

'Well, you know Geordie Ron . . .?' she began.

'Yes . . .' I said curiously, wondering how he fitted into all this. Then realisation hit me in the stomach.

'Oh no!'

'Oh Barry, he's so lovely. He's been everywhere and done everything. He's just so . . . so terrific!' she babbled. 'I'm meeting him after work.'

I kept my own opinion of Ron to myself but I sensed trouble. Not only was Jo my closest friend on the island, she was also the person I relied on at work, so the last thing I wanted was him upsetting her. I said nothing and we went to work. We had a very successful evening and by the end of the night I was in high spirits. Ron hadn't been mentioned and I was beginning to suspect that I had imagined the whole episode, when suddenly, there he was, waiting for us in the last bar. He had obviously stolen some clothes and an iron from somewhere because he looked quite presentable in a '70s sort of way. When he caught sight of me and Jo coming into the bar his face lit up with well-rehearsed ecstasy. He bounded over to her like a big daft St Bernard.

'And how's my favourite chick, then?' he oozed.

'All the better for seeing you, babes,' she fawned back.

'OK. Well, let's blow this joint and get down to some serious lovin',' he announced through his cheap sunglasses.

I winced. Had this man slipped through a loophole in the space-time continuum? I decided to find out.

'Excuse me, are you from1970?' I inquired politely.

'Aha yeah, good one that. Very funny,' said Ron, unsure how to take me.

He eyed me up and down. I could see the mental processes taking place as he weighed up his options and chose, for now at least, to try and befriend me, given that I was a lifelong friend of Joanne.

With this protective shield in place I decided to press on.

'Only, your shirt is unbuttoned to the waist, and you're wearing rather a large medallion,' I pointed out cheerfully.

Ron didn't miss a beat. He wasn't going to get angry in front of

Joanne until he had established a relationship. There would be plenty of time for violence later.

'Ha ha, you're a card aren't you? He's a card isn't he Jo?' he smiled gratingly.

'Yeah, he's a card all right,' said Jo, shooting me a warning glance and squeezing Ron's hand.

It was at that moment that I knew that he was on the scene to stay.

After that it was just a matter of time. Soon they had moved in together. Then they arrived arm in arm a few weeks later at a photo meeting.

'Hello, Ron,' I said. 'Have you been promoted to the photo team?'

Ron was looking extremely pleased with himself as Jo guiltily began talking.

'Erm, actually Barry, that's something we wanted to talk to you about.'

'Go on,' I said warily.

'Well, Jo and I feel that since we're so much in love, I should be there to support her at work,' said Ron.

Support her in what sense? I wondered. Was he going to carry her round the bars? He was a crap OPC.

'Barry, we want to give it a shot working together,' Jo explained tentatively, studying my face for a reaction.

My reaction was forceful.

'How can you?' I exploded. 'We're a team, Jo, we work well together. Look how tough it was to get all the best bars. Surely you don't want to give all that up?'

'Oh yes, your bars. That's another subject we wanted to discuss,' smirked Ron.

'What!' I cried, my carefully constructed world was being torn asunder. Ron explained his theory that since I was such a good OPC, I would still be able to get ups, even out of quiet bars. Whereas he, as a beginner, deserved a break and ought to have Jo and I's busy ones.

'Anyway, Jo gets on well with the bar owners and she'll help me settle in,' he told me as though I would give a shit.

'Settle in, my arse!' I roared. 'I'm telling Pete. There's no way I'm giving up my bars to you.'

Ron had anticipated my reaction, however, and his closing argument to Pete was that under the new arrangement Jo would be getting as many couples with him as she was with me. I on the other hand would have to work harder, but obviously would still do well in my new bars. Thus Pete would make more money. Upon hearing the 'more money' part of Ron's speech, Pete's mind was made up. Ron and Jo were given the good bars that we had fought so hard to acquire. I was given some quiet seafront bars and paired up with a sneaky Dutchman called Tom. We did OK, but not as well as before. It was to be the beginning of my disillusionment with Oasis Beach Club.

Tom was an interesting companion and we quickly became friends. He was twenty-one, which to me meant that he was a man of the world. He was taller than me and sported a pristine-looking flat-top, influenced, I suspected, by Alex. A meticulous dresser, he was also very calculating in his approach to life in general. The sort of chap who never embarked on a course of action without anticipating every possible consequence. He introduced me to marijuana and one evening undertook to show me the inside of a brothel. I had never been in one before and it was a real eye-opener. I had kind of expected a harem of beautiful, exotic women parading themselves invitingly while we sipped cocktails. The reality was a twenty five quid cup of warm beer and an ugly dwarf making lewd suggestions in Spanish. After fending her off and abandoning my cup of beer we beat a hasty retreat to an all night café. It was there that we began to discuss plans for our futures.

Tom, it transpired, was also not happy with Oasis and had been having drinks with the project director of a rival company. Jock McLeod was his name, he ran a timeshare called the Mayfair Club and had recently approached Tom with a view to recruiting him. Jock wanted him to set up a photo team for Mayfair and was prepared to pay. Tom asked me what I thought about us sharing the job.

We discussed the wisdom of leaving Oasis. The pros were obvious. Management positions, good money and more free time to enjoy it. The cons were that Pete and Alex had always made it quite plain that anyone attempting to leave and work for another company, would be beaten to the point of hospitalisation. Their back and legs would be slashed with a razor and they would be forcibly ejected from the island.

It was six and two threes. We agreed to call on Jock and see what he had to say.

The Mayfair Club was right next door to Oasis and rivalled it for beauty and luxury. It was very nearly as successful and they desperately wanted a photo team. Jock wined and dined us while he picked our brains and eventually it was time to make a decision. The offer on the table was a grand each starting money, our own cars, an apartment between us, an override of ten pounds per couple on the work of a pre-recruited team and fifty pounds on each of their deals. For this we would have to recruit new bars to work in, negotiate a deal with a photo studio who were capable of doing all the developing and framing work and train and run the team.

Yes, yes, yes, we thought, all very well, but what about our personal safety?

'No problem,' said Jock, 'we're protected by the Italian Mafia and the club owner, Manelli, has said he'll provide you with an armed bodyguard while you work for us.'

We believed him. We were hooked. All of our concerns seemed to have been answered and we were going to be the youngest team captains on the island.

'Jock, you've got yourself a deal!' I announced. We all shook hands. Jock paid the bill and we arranged to meet in his office after the weekend.

After the initial self-congratulations and euphoria had worn off, we remembered that we still had the immediate problem of facing Pete and Alex before we were assigned our bodyguard. Following some agitated discussion, we settled on the idea of going to Oasis and officially resigning. It would be better than living in fear and this way we would be able to gauge the reactions of Pete and Alex when we told them.

Hard on the heels of this decision, came the realisation that their reactions were going to be extremely violent.

Tom was pacing up and down.

'We're going to need a gun,' he declared solemnly.

'What the fuck are you talking about?' I asked, worried.

'And some C.S. gas,' he continued, warming to his theme.

His eyes had gone all intense and the veins on the side of his neck had started to pulsate.

'Christ on a bike!' I spluttered.

'It's going to be a two-man operation,' he explained. 'You shoot Alex first, then cover me while I . . .'

'I'm not bloody-well going to shoot anybody,' I shouted. 'Get a hold of yourself, you fucking lunatic!'

I was extremely anxious about these previously unrevealed personality traits of the man I was about to go into business with but, after some consideration, I opted to dismiss it as a one-off. Just to be sure, I thought I would give him a lecture.

'Tom look, we're only young lads. I'm nineteen, you're twenty-one. Let's not go getting out of our depth here OK? Now, are we going to be sensible about this?' I nodded, encouraging him to agree.

'You don't understand Barry. It's them or us and we've got to hit them first!'

'Now stop it!' I yelled firmly, ready to lose control.

Subdued, Tom agreed that we shouldn't kill anybody but in the end even I had to admit that I didn't fancy facing the big fellas unprotected. We compromised. We bought a revolver from a waiter in one of our bars and a small canister of C.S. gas from a security guard I knew.

The plan was that we would go into Oasis Beach Club with the weapons concealed and find Pete and Alex at a time when they were likely to be together, in order to resign. That way, if things did turn ugly, we could use the C.S. gas and run. If any razors appeared, then one of us would have to shoot them in the legs. We flipped a coin and Tom won the dubious honour of carrying the gun. Manfully, he concealed it in his jacket. I tucked the little gas canister into my shirt sleeve and we set off.

The marketing office at Oasis looked larger and more imposing than it usually did. We stood around for a bit, then took the plunge and knocked. The door swung open as we rapped, to reveal Alex on his own, sitting with his feet up on the desk. We quickly glanced around for Pete but he wasn't in the room.

Alex turned towards us.

'So! Butch and Sundance,' he said. 'Come to resign then have you?'

I froze. How had he known that we were going to resign? And the Butch and Sundance reference seemed to suggest, alarmingly, that he also knew we had a gun. Before losing total control of the situation, I ploughed on.

'Er . . . yeah! We're going to work for Mayfair, Alex.'

At last it was out in the open. No going back now! Alex clasped his club-like hands together and lowered his feet to the floor. He inclined his head in contemplation. Finally he spoke.

'You know we're not going to let you do that,' he quietly warned.

'Our minds are made up . . . ' Tom started.

'Yes, Jock has made us a good offer and we have to take it,' I interjected rapidly, fearing that Tom might start slipping back into his street warrior role and do something we would both regret.

Alex's eyes flicked back and forth between me and Tom, observing the interplay.

'OK boys, do what you gotta do!' he said finally. 'I'm not going to do anything until Pete gets back from England. Then we're coming after you. And you're getting it!' He frowned for a moment, then said, 'Off you go.'

Off we went. Hmm, I thought to myself as we drove off, only a partial success! I pretended to need the toilet as an excuse to stop the car when we driven out of town. As I was getting out I snatched the gun from Tom and bolted from the vehicle. I managed to throw it over the cliff edge and into the sea before Tom caught up with me. He was livid, but as I told him, we weren't going to shoot anyone. All that gun was going to do was get us in trouble. Eventually he agreed that the best thing we could do was to move into our new apartment and keep our heads down until we got our bodyguard.

Jock was as good as his word in that respect. Alphonso was waiting for us, playing with his shooter, when we turned up for our first day at the Mayfair Club – he would be our protection of an evening, as we worked the bars. Tom and I got down to business straightaway. We recruited over fifty new bars and trained up eleven teams to operating capacity, all before Pete got back from the UK. Alphonso was in tow all the time we were at work, looking as menacing as he could. In the daytime we just hid in the house. This arrangement gave us peace of mind concerning our security but it was no way to live. Eventually, we heard that Pete was back and we chose to risk going into town. We had to see Pete sometime and we reasoned that he wasn't going to do anything to us in public.

We were wrong. No sooner had we driven into town than we heard the frantic beeping of a motorbike horn.

'Oh shit, it's him,' I grimaced, looking at the familiar sight of muscles, baseball cap and angry red motorbike in my rearview mirror. He was motioning vigorously for us to pull over. I couldn't see a knife or razor, so I made the decision to pull over at the busy Bouganville hotel boardwalk, outside the police station and beside the taxi rank.

'We'll be safe here,' I reassured Tom.

'Ugh, ugh, help!' he replied.

Odd answer, I thought and turned to find Pete pulling Tom out of the car window. On hearing his screams of pain I sprang out of the vehicle and immediately darted to safety.

'Use the C.S. gas, Tom!' I shouted from behind the car. 'Spray him and run away!'

Tom was already unconscious but Pete carried on pounding his limp form anyway for a few minutes just to make sure. Then he picked up what looked to me like Tom's corpse and started shaking it.

'Where's your gun?' he demanded. 'Because I'm going to shove it up your arse!'

Eliciting no response from the mangled wreck of Tom, he dropped him and turned his attention to me.

'Come here you!' he roared. 'It's your turn!'

'Bollocks to that!' I yelled over my shoulder as I dodged round the car. 'You can fucking whistle mate!'

Pete feinted this way and that but I managed to keep the car firmly between us. To a passer-by it must have looked quite amusing but, what with my life being at stake, I chose to take it seriously. Eventually Pete seemed to calm down a bit. He stopped chasing and stood eyeballing me across the roof of the vehicle as he caught his breath.

'I ought to catch you and maim you,' he said, 'but seeing as how it was Tom who had the gun, I'm going to let you go. As long as you both leave the island today.'

It seemed fair enough to me.

'We're out of here,' I told him. 'No problem!'

Pete told me that he wanted us to go and buy our tickets off the island immediately. If we didn't show them to him within the hour, then our amnesty would be void and we would both be leaving the island in boxes. Then, still keeping the car between us, I watched him jump on his motorbike and speed off. I turned to see a couple of policemen stepping disinterestedly over Tom before I scooped him up and poured him onto the back seat.

'Come on, Tom, we're leaving,' I said as we drove off.

Tom woke up about 45 minutes later as I finished packing our stuff.

'Ow! my whole body is in pain,' he said. 'Why didn't you help me?'

Wasn't it obvious?

'I might have been hurt, Tom,' I explained, 'and I don't think either of us would have wanted that!'

We rang Jock and resigned. He promised to get us a job

somewhere else. A couple of phone calls later, that 'somewhere else' turned out to be Gran Canaria. Jock had a mate who ran a timeshare resort over there and he wanted a photo team. Jock told us that the guy was offering us the same deal as he had done. After buying the tickets we drove directly to Oasis to show Pete. He was outside the main reception chatting to Alex. I displayed the tickets to him through the closed window, my thumb firmly on the door lock. Pete examined them and nodded.

'You can wind your window down, I'm not going to hurt you,' he said.

Yeah right, I thought and checked to make sure that Tom's door was locked too. Pete looked at me.

'Barry, I don't blame you for trying. You just chose the wrong bloke to go up against, that's all. Good luck in GC.'

With that, he waved us off out of there, and on to Gran Canaria!

# 3

# GRAN CANARIA

Gran Canaria is the third-largest Canary Island after Tenerife and Lanzerote. Timeshare is also prevalent here and the set up was pretty similar except that there was a good deal less criminal involvement. The companies in GC seemed to be of the interesting opinion that business should be conducted along the lines of hard work and trust. It wouldn't take long for them to wake up and smell the coffee. The reason why violence was a necessary part of everyday life in the industry was two-pronged. Firstly, the nature of OPCs is that they can be fickle with their loyalty, where cash is concerned. The only way that companies held on to their OPC teams was to pay good wages. This could often mean that a five pound hike in the price of a couple by the company next door would spark a mass exodus of your entire team. Things did actually spiral out of control for a time and several companies went out of business trying to keep up with extortionate wage demands. After a while, some of the wiser heads at the helms of the firms in Tenerife came up with the cross-hire agreement. This was an initiative under which no firm would take on an OPC who had left another company on the same island, for a period of three months after termination of employment. When stuck to, this agreement helped the companies to regain a measure of control in the marketplace. Naturally there were those who circumvented the rules, undermining the effectiveness of the agreement, so that the only option left to companies was to play hardball. Every company worth its salt began hiring muscle, or clumpers.

The other, and perhaps deciding factor in the industry's decision to bring in the heavies was that everybody was working illegally and in many ways beyond the reach of the law. In the absence of any outside policing we had to police ourselves. The role of the clumper was manifold. They handled internal discipline and enforced verbal work contracts. But they would also protect the workforce from outside threat, such as irate tourists or OPCs from other companies trying to steal our business.

Tom and I knew that all this had yet to happen in Gran Canaria and the fact that the island was still pleasantly clumper free was a major influence on our decision to choose it for our new theatre of operations.

We landed in the middle of the night after a twenty-minute flight from 'The Grief', as we used to call Tenerife. The half-hour taxi ride from the airport was paid for by the receptionist at the company accommodation. Tom and I dumped our bags at the villa, found out where the nearest bars were and went on the piss.

We met the boss the next afternoon. His name was John and, try as he might, he was having trouble believing that Jock was doing him a favour. No project director gave away OPCs, especially without demanding money for them.

Even after we explained the situation properly to him, he told us he was still suspicious. He also told us that we would get no 'starting' money until he 'started' seeing results from the photo team we set up for him.

This threw us a bit. We were expecting the cash straightaway. We were in no position to argue, so we agreed that he was right and that this was the only fair way to do it. Then we explained that we would need a float of a thousand pounds to get 'started'.

'You know, to buy cameras,' I said.

'And pay bars,' added Tom.

'Not to mention the photo studio,' I reminded him.

'Oh yes, got to pay the photo studio,' Tom agreed.

'All kinds of expenses,' I concluded.

'Some of them unforeseen,' Tom nodded.

John gave in.

'OK OK, you can have your float money, but I want receipts for everything. I'm sure you wouldn't rip me off for a lousy grand now, would you lads?'

Such an extraordinary lack of judgement hardly gave us grounds for confidence but we decided to give the place a chance before running off with the money.

We got up the next afternoon and recruited a few bars and restaurants but, to be honest, the place didn't really grow on us. After a few days of half-hearted effort, out of the blue, I remembered that my dad was due to be visiting me in Tenerife. That day, in fact. He had booked the holiday ages ago and given me plenty of notice. Now, with the confusion of the last few days, I had forgotten to phone him and let him know that I had left the island. In a panic I informed Tom.

'What am I going to do?' I demanded of him. 'He'll have already set off by now!'

All we could think of was to leave a message at Tenerife airport for my father to catch another plane to Gran Canaria as soon as he got there. We could meet him and take him back to our company apartment. I was wishing that I could give him a better holiday, given that it was to be the first time he had visited me since I had moved abroad.

Still, you play the cards you are dealt. Tom and I rang Tenerife airport and, in our broken Spanish, left what we hoped was a message for my dad to take the next plane to GC.

I was a little nervous during the journey to meet him. My father is an ex-RAF officer and is used to planning events with military precision down to the last detail. I knew that he would probably be expecting a conventional 'father-visits-successful-son-working-abroad' type of a holiday. Possibly including meeting with my colleagues, visiting my work and maybe even a few pleasant evenings spent in good company at my favourite restaurants.

I was well aware, therefore, that island hopping to avoid death threats by Pete and Alex would be fairly low on his itinerary. It wasn't the ideal situation, but needs must when the devil farts in your tent. I just hoped that Dad had got the message we had left for him at the airport.

He had indeed. Tom and I turned up to Las Palmas airport a few hours later, intending to meet every plane from Tenerife that Dad could have connected with. Full credit to the man, he hadn't missed a beat. Upon receiving the message from airport control, he had calmly and efficiently booked himself on the next flight over to us. As we pulled up in our company car, the airport was deserted except for my father, who was sitting on his suitcase scanning the horizon for us with one hand shielding his eyes from the sun.

His behaviour was impeccable as we sheepishly greeted him.

'Hiya son, how's business?' he inquired, graciously ignoring my failure to warn him of the rather significant changes to his travel plans.

'Oh, you know, not too bad. A few minor difficulties avoiding homicidal gangsters but apart from that, everything's fine.'

I attempted to gloss over the problems so as not to worry him.

'How was your flight anyway, Dad?'

'Great, thanks, I caught the connection in Tenerife without too much delay. Homicidal gangsters you say?'

'Really, there's nothing to worry about,' I assured him. 'Come on, I bet you can't wait to get back to the apartment for a shower.'

Dad left it at that, so we went home and got him unpacked.

After an afternoon on the beach, we went for a meal at a seafront restaurant. We had a relaxed evening and Dad hadn't inquired further about why we had left Tenerife. I was actually beginning to believe that I wasn't going to have to furnish a more in-depth explanation, when over the brandies he gently began his interrogation.

'So, what is it that you're not telling me, boys?' he asked jovially.

'About what?' I feigned surprise.

'Well, you left good jobs, fled Tenerife in the middle of the night and I believe you mentioned homicidal gangsters?' he summarised plainly.

I knew I was defeated. Long experience of failed attempts to hide the truth from this man had taught me the futility of trying.

Suddenly I was twelve years old again, holding a dodgy school report card behind my back. I knew I would have to cough up sooner or later, so I explained the entire situation to him. His eyebrows went up a little when I told him about the revolver and C.S. gas, but went back down again when he heard how we escaped without using them.

'All's well that ends well,' he concluded. 'Presumably you've learnt your lesson and will be behaving yourselves from now on?'

I looked at Tom. Tom looked at the ground. There was one more piece of bad news to break and Tom was obviously leaving the breaking to me. I took a deep breath and began.

I nodded sagely, agreeing that yes, we had learned our lesson and would, as he said, be behaving ourselves from now on. As soon as we had done a runner with the thousand pounds we were about to steal from the current timeshare baron.

Dad began to express his reservations but I wasn't finished. I was on a confessional roll and took the opportunity to drop the bombshell that Tom and I's first performance meeting was due in a couple of days. As we didn't have any receipts to show for the money we had taken, we would have to disappear before that.

Dad was naturally more than a little put out at being involved, by implication, in our scam. Even so he was supportive and offered his military expertise in helping us plan our escape.

This was going to be tricky because we were actually staying on the timeshare complex we were working for. The receptionists would be sure to tell John if the two new team captains were catching a taxi to the airport with all their suitcases, so soon after arriving.

We decided to leave in the middle of the night for Tenerife and to see whether Pete and Alex had relented in their attitude towards us. The next night was chosen for the operation. Dad sunbathed by the pool all day as Tom and I drove around keeping up appearances. That evening we went out for a meal with John, during the course of which Dad guiltily shifted food around on his plate while Tom and I happily discussed expansion plans for the photo team with the gaffer. Afterwards we went back to the apartment. We all packed our bags. Then I left a note on the coffee table explaining our decision to leave due to unforeseen circumstances. I justified the missing thousand pounds with a list of costs. Consultancy fees, time spent recruiting, petrol money and miscellaneous expenses. Our total fee actually worked out to be one thousand and five pounds and twenty pence, but I told John to forget about the change.

Our consciences cleared, we all went to bed. At three o'clock in the morning, Tom's alarm clock woke us and we crept past the reception, luggage and all, to our waiting taxi.

Three hours later we were checking into a hotel in Los Christianos in South Tenerife.

# 4

# TENERIFE II

We stayed in this hotel until Dad flew back to England. It was a different town to Pete and Alex, so we were relatively safe. At least we had a few days' holiday with my father before he left and we tried to use this time to reassure him that we would be OK. Saying goodbye to him, I made a mental resolution that I would get my situation more stable before his next visit.

Down to business again. Tom and I went to see Jock, to find out if there was any way he could wangle our protection in order that we could work for him again.

On the phone, Jock was very confidant. He said that the owner of the Mayfair Club, Manelli, was currently on the island and that he wanted to see us. We were interested. Jock had previously told us that Manelli was a *bona fide* member of the Sicilian Mafia. In addition to the fact that, in theory at least, he should be able to offer us protection from Pete and Alex, we wanted to meet him anyway. Not many of our friends back home in England and Holland could boast wise-guys among their acquaintances.

Before the meeting we dressed up in what we thought was appropriate: sharp lightweight suits, sunglasses and briefcases. Tom drew the line at fedora hats but even so, we thought we would fit in with the most hardened circle of mobsters.

The meeting was in Manelli's office and, as the events of that day were to unfold, far from 'observing the power of Manelli', as the Italian-suited businessman had so confidently predicted, so began our dramatic journey to flee the island – to England, and to safety.

For the next day or so we did not really give our situation much thought. We travelled from Manchester via trains and buses to my Dad's house in a little Yorkshire village called Dalton (my mother and father had separated and my mum now lived in the Lake District). Even though we had neglected to warn him of our arrival, he didn't seem in the least surprised to see us.

'I've made beds up for you boys,' he smiled. 'I thought you might turn up here soon.'

We muttered our thanks and trudged upstairs to unpack. It gave me a strange sense of well-being to be back in my old bedroom and for a good half an hour or so I lay on my bed, looking at the familiar ceiling, until I eventually dozed off.

I woke up around teatime and after a shower I met Tom down in the kitchen. He had already made friends with my brother Jim, who had just come home from school. Dad's girlfriend cooked us all a meal and, while we ate, they questioned us about our escapades. We answered as truthfully as the situation allowed, skimming over some of the nastier details. For fun I was telling Tom to go fuck his mother in Dutch, in a pleasant voice whilst pointing at the saltpot. No-one sussed me, except Tom, of course, who went redder than a beetroot. This method of winding Tom up infuriated him throughout our time in England. Smilingly talking gutter-Dutch to him while in the company of decent non-comprehending members of my family and friends.

After the meal we finally began to take stock of our situation. We had about two and a half grand each, we were unable to return to at least two of the seven Canary Islands and we didn't have any idea what to do next. On the plus side, we weren't scared to try new places and, while we figured out where to go, we were welcome at my dad's house.

The days stretched into weeks, spent drinking with my old friends in town and with my relatives at my uncle's pub in the village. After a while, Tom decided he wanted to go back to Holland and pursue some kind of career. I took him to the airport and when we said goodbye it was the last time I ever saw him. Although about a month later he rang me to say that he'd secured a good job in advertising, replete with flash company car.

With my money dwindling, I realised that it was time to travel. I wanted to get involved in the timeshare game again because I knew it was an easy way for me to make money. First came the job of selecting a new henchman. One of my pals from school told me he was up for a bit of adventure. His name was Chris. He had always been one of the outgoing members of our crowd and was the only one I knew with the balls to risk going to live in another country.

Having agreed to team up, we decided to ask Jock's advice on where to go. I hadn't spoken to him since leaving Tenerife the last time. He didn't sound over pleased to hear from me. Apparently, Pete and Alex's rage at Tom and I's escape had been vented on him when Alex's motorbike was found knocked over.

Eventually though, after a bombardment of phone calls, he suggested that we try his friend who ran a timeshare on the Costa del Sol.

We phoned the number that Jock gave us but there was no reply. Fuck it, we thought, and caught the next available plane anyway.

# 5

# THE COSTA DEL SOL

Malaga looked beautiful as we flew over it at sunset. After landing we had to get a bus down to Benelmadena and check into a hostel. We knew we would have to find the timeshare in the daytime during business hours. The most productive thing we could do that night was go out and get bladdered, so we did.

We got back into the hostel the next day, minutes before it was time to check out. There is no comparably dreadful feeling quite like staggering around with heavy luggage in blinding sunlight, nursing a stonking great hangover. Nevertheless, we struggled on. We got on a bus to Marbella, where the Riu Palace timeshare was. We were fully expecting Hassan, Jock's friend, to welcome us with open arms, give us a job and usher us to some free accommodation. We got to the reception and collapsed on the leather chairs.

The receptionist glared at us. To be fair to her, we probably looked pretty bad but I told her that Hassan would understand when I explained to him that we had been travelling for a couple of days to get there.

'Hassan who?' inquired the receptionist disbelievingly.

'Er, isn't he the marketing manager here?' I asked.

'No.'

'Let me get this straight,' I was getting alarmed by now. 'You haven't heard of him?'

'No. And I'd like you both to leave!'

It transpired upon further enquiry that yes, there had been a chap called Hassan working there six months ago but that he had long since been arrested for fraud and was currently in jail. He sounds like one of Jock's friends right enough, I thought grimly. We headed despondently to another hostel and checked in.

We were feeling more than a little bit miffed but now wasn't the time to dwell on our bad luck. We had to get jobs, and fast. We decided we would have to work as street OPCs, at least until we could find a company that wanted a photo team.

The OPCs on the Costa were all about ten years older than us and seemed to think that we were too young to be over there without our mums. After enduring some tedious jokes about youth opportunity schemes, we persuaded a couple of them to introduce us to their manager.

His name was Steve and he worked for Benelmadena Beach Club. After a brief tour of the resort he issued us with tickets, dumped us on San Miguel Street in Torremolinos and told us to get to work.

We tried, but I hadn't worked the street for so long that I had forgotten just how hard it was. For Chris it was even worse, because being new to the OPC game, he had never done any of it before. We soon gave up. That night we went round the bars and found a job PRing. I say 'a' job because there was only one. We had to share it. It paid a tenner a night which meant a fiver each, plus free drinks. All we had to do was stand on the main strip and blag tourists into a bar. Amazingly enough we lasted for three weeks doing this job. There was no pressure, our life solely consisted of drinking and seducing young female tourists. Notably enough we hardly ever slept with the girls that worked for the other bars, they were only interested in the tourists, too. A tenner, it turned out, was enough to pay for the hostel and eat. Daytimes were spent sleeping, either in the hostel or on the beach. Marijuana was very cheap on the Costa because Morocco was so close, and this was the cause of my first argument with Chris. The money we had brought with us soon ran out and our wages were finely balanced between buying food and buying drugs. One afternoon, when neither of us had eaten all day, Chris set off with our last fiver to buy some food. I was starving but Chris did not reappear until just before it was time to go to work. He had a sheepish grin on his face and when I demanded food he told me that he had spent the money on hash. I went berserk and we had an almighty row. I accused him of being irresponsible and he blamed me for dragging him away from England. I pointed out that, either way, we still had nothing to eat for another twelve hours.

Eventually we calmed down and reasoned that our only option was to fill up on the free beer from work. This would have to last us until such time as we could afford to buy some food. This particular incident brought home to me the fact that we were completely skint and I realised that we would have to get back into timeshare pretty smart if we were going to get out of this rut.

Yet again Lady Luck stepped in. Wandering past our bar that night came an ex-manager from Oasis Beach Club called Carlos. Oasis, as you will recall, was the first company I worked for in Tenerife. Carlos had worked for the Costa del Sol division and had recently got financial backing to set up his own timeshare company in Fuengirola. He needed OPCs. He didn't care about my bad record in Tenerife and gave us both jobs on the spot. We got one month's free accommodation and a car for the same period.

Yippee, we thought. This certainly took some of the immediate pressure off and, additionally, he promised to pay us daily instead of weekly until we got back on our feet. He also gave us the prime location to work: on the beachwalk, ten metres from the entrance to his club, called 'The Girolamar'. This was a real bonus because instead of having to send couples on to the timeshare in taxis, which sometimes made them nervous, we could simply walk them through the door.

We moved into our free apartment the next morning. It was excellent. Smoked-glass tables, barbeque on the verandah, even a father-figure-type Swedish guy called Ken to share with. He was extremely knowledgeable, compared to us, in that he was able to cook and could get a week's worth of food for next to nothing by shopping carefully. He was about forty years old and was now teetotal following a period as an alcoholic. Heaving drunk away two businesses he had managed to beat the booze and these days he was was fit, healthy and successful. This was another point of contention between myself and Chris – he found it funny to keep offering Ken beers, whereas I did not.

We started work on the same day that we moved in. I found that being surrounded by the friendly crowd of young OPCs who were working for Girolamar helped me enormously and I did much better. I got four or five ups on the first day and Chris also performed well. We settled into a nice routine working for Carlos. Suddenly we had money again – which, true to form, we duly wasted. Most of it went on booze and experimenting with drugs. I won't attempt to glamorise drug use – I have had my share of nightmare experiences over the years and thrown an awful lot of money away. On the whole I am probably lucky to be alive but I would be skipping parts of my story if I failed to write about certain chemical escapades. Smoking hash is pretty common among my generation and is not really worth mentioning here. On the Costa at this time, the recreational pharmaceuticals that proved most popular were acid and speed.

The first time we dabbled, we were in a club in Fuengirola. It was about three o'clock in the morning, we were very drunk and the place was just beginning to liven up. A friend of ours mentioned that she had some trips and would we like some? We took one each and after a few minutes, experiencing no reaction, we had another. What we didn't realise was that acid only starts working approximately forty minutes after it has been ingested. Anyway, ten minutes later we were still getting no result so we had two more.

'This is shit!' I told Chris. 'I can't see what all the fuss is about.'

'Maybe we just haven't had enough,' Chris reasoned. 'Let's try a few more.'

After about six trips each we still felt nothing, so we decided to have some speed instead. We swallowed a gram each and started smoking a spliff.

'Nope, nothing yet,' Chris complained.

'It must be the atmosphere,' I said. 'Let's go to Torremolinos. I bet that if everyone around us is having a good time it will rub off on us.'

Chris agreed that moving to a livelier location might stimulate the drugs into working.

The road from Fuengirola to Torremolinos at that time was officially the most dangerous strip of motorway in Europe. More people used to die in accidents each year on this road than any other on the continent.

'Let's drive there!' was our rather foolish plan.

While some people believe that a guardian angel looks after drunks and small children, we were pretty sure that the self-same angel must also have a soft spot for drugged-up idiots. Either that or we were just bloody lucky. I was gradually losing touch with reality as I steered the car at breakneck speed. We flew round hairpin bends along the cliff edges that are a feature of the Costa del Sol. I could not honestly tell you how we survived the experience. During most of the journey I was unaware that it was me who was driving the vehicle. I was merrily zooming through an alternate universe at well over 100 miles an hour, when Chris began punching me in the kidneys. Gradually his words penetrated the dense fog around my brain.

'Barry, slow down, for fuck's sake. There's a police road block ahead!'

I turned to face the source of his agitation and began to feel nervous. There were four or five sinister-looking members of the Guardia Civil standing in the road up ahead. They motioned for us to pull over with their glowing traffic batons. I became even more uneasy when I noticed that they had machine-guns and vicious-looking dogs. These were probably only Alsatians but they appeared far more distorted and terrifying because of the drugs. We stopped and were pulled from the car to be searched. Then the dogs were led into the vehicle for a sniff around. One came out with a big joint triumphantly clamped between its teeth. This upped the tempo considerably. The officers started barking questions at us in Spanish – our reply to which involved giggling uncontrollably and pulling faces at them. Somewhere in the back of my mind, however, the idea was beginning to filter through that we might be in a spot of bother here. One copper was holding the spliff an inch in front of my face and angrily shouting something at me. In my diminished state of reason I interpreted his words as a request for a light, and solemnly offered him my lighter. Chris saw me and collapsed on the floor with laughter. It was infectious and, when I realised what I was doing, I did too.

I will never understand why they let us go. Maybe it was sheer exasperation. Whatever the reason, after twenty minutes or so of this sort of nonsense the police pushed us back into the car, turned the ignition on, shut the doors and motioned us on our way.

Of all the occasions where people have been stopped for dangerous driving at night by the police, I can't think of one occasion where the officers in question would have been more justified in throwing the offenders straight into jail. In the end I think they decided that it wasn't worth the aggravation. They probably wanted us to crash and learn our lesson that way.

We didn't crash, and having survived our first serious encounter with drugs, they became a fairly regular feature of nights out during the next few years. These days I am older and prefer to be in control a little more, well, to the extent that you can be in control when drinking alcohol.

We were, by now, thoroughly enjoying ourselves on the Costa. Work was paying well, and a few friends of mine from the Canary Islands had shown up in Fuengirola. Most notably, an Indian girl called Jacky – perhaps one of the most pushy and persuasive of people I've ever met. The timeshare business is full of big egos and I have worked with many outstanding OPCs. Many, if not all of them, might have claimed to be the best – they would have been wrong, that particular crown always belonged to Jacky. This was a girl who set records wherever she went for getting the most ups in a week. At the age of 21, she was regularly earning pay cheques of two thousand pounds a week. She owned apartments, businesses and a Porsche. I used to try and work near her as often as possible, in the hope that some of the magic might rub off on me. Jacky was travelling with a group of Scandinavians and they sold themselves as a team to our company. They totalled six in all and were a very pleasant bunch, too. Chris and I became good mates with them and soon they asked us to join their team. They had formed something called an 'up shop'. What this basically meant was that they acted as free agents. They would move from company to company, staying until the free accommodation and car had run out before they moved on. They also managed themselves, meaning that they got more money for their couples because the companies they worked for did not have the expense of paying an override to a manager. So as our boss, Carlos, had never opted to retain the services of a clumper, when our free housing ran out at Girolamar, Chris and I willingly moved on with Jacky and her gang. We worked for seven different companies in as many months, always enjoying free villas and cars.

It was during this period that we met two journalists from one of the largest British Sunday newspapers. I was working outside a resort called Club Puerto Banus one day when I saw an attractive young couple looking a bit lost. Pulling my cap straight I darted over to pitch them. I had just started my speech when the woman had the cheek to interrupt me.

'Actually, we're reporters,' she told me, and went on to name the paper.

It was one of the more notorious scandalmonger papers and I was suitably impressed. We got chatting and they told me that they were doing an article on married women who came on singles holidays to the Costa to sleep with the British workers there. I made a deal with them that they could use me in their story if they had a look around my timeshare. This particular club was paying us thirty-five pounds an up and the reporters agreed to do it. Different timeshare companies have different rules. Some will pay the OPC as soon as the couple goes through reception, whereas others will only pay after the up has been on tour with a sales person for twenty, thirty or sixty minutes. Luckily, Club Puerto Banus paid immediately, because the reporters came running out after a minute and a half.

Jacky and the others turned up as I was having coffee with the reporters afterwards. Their names were Jan and Andy and they took us all for lunch, during the course of which they regaled us with tales of journalistic coups they had pulled off. It was an awesome list. Three out of four of the biggest headlines that I could think of in the last ten years had been Jan's. While we ate and chatted about timeshare, I noticed that they had left their dictaphone running. Thinking that she had left it on by accident, I pointed it out to her so that she could save her batteries. She said thanks and turned it off, but the look on her face was strange and I mentally recorded the incident.

The story that they claimed to want (about married women coming down to the Costa to chase male OPCs and PRs) did not seem to be working out for them, so Chris and I were prevailed upon to deliver some juicy stories. We duly invented some gruesome sexual escapades for them to sensationalise. They were impressed and told us that the story would be printed in the paper in a few weeks' time. We thought no more about it.

For the rest of that week, Jan and Andy knocked about with us. They had a seemingly bottomless expense account, which they weren't shy about dipping into. We ate in the best restaurants and drank in the most expensive bars in Puerto Banus. At one point during the week, they took some photographs of Chris and me on the beach holding jugs of sangria, with our arms around a couple of topless beach beauties.

When the time came for them to leave, they had interviewed everyone from drug dealers to timeshare barons and we expected the story to involve some kind of scandal. When it came out, however, I was completely unprepared for the impact it was going to have on my relationship with my co-conspirators in the Costa del Sol timeshare game.

The article wasn't due out for another month and, in the meantime, interesting developments were taking place. Ben Hinks, the guy who had first shown me how to OPC, had arrived on the Costa. He had been driving around with a big Cockney bloke called Jim, looking at all the different timeshare resorts. I had taken him to meet Carlos and, after some negotiation, Ben and Jim took over the marketing of Girolamar and were now working directly under

Carlos. This meant that they had overall responsibility for every OPC in the company. I immediately got myself reinstated at Girolamar along with Chris. Jacky and the others left to work another town, so we split up with them for the time being.

Working for Ben was excellent because he didn't mind throwing his money around in order to keep his workforce happy. He would regularly take us out drinking, or to the go-karts, or waterskiing, and pay for it all. In doing this he kept us motivated and ensured our loyalty.

Ben had quite a task on his hands trying to keep me out of trouble with the American owners of the company who had put up the initial money for Carlos to develop Girolamar. You see, I was getting a bit of a reputation for blagging the ups. It's obviously much easier to lie to a couple about where you're taking them than it is to tell them they're going to visit a timeshare. The trouble is, when they realise that they've been conned, they can become bad tempered and sometimes even bad tempered violent, which makes it a lot more difficult for the poor salesperson trying to sell to them. Not that I cared, I got paid just for getting them there. Blagging was par for the course as far as I was concerned. As usual though, I went too far. I would tell people that there was a free beer promotion from San Miguel, or a dolphin show, or underwater bull fighting or anything else if it meant that they would walk through the reception door.

Things came to a head when the directors discovered that I had been enlisting the help of a pair of small children who were staying at the club. I was working the beachwalk outside reception one day when I noticed a little boy and girl of about four and six hanging around the ice-cream counter of the complex restaurant. After befriending them I hit upon a brilliant new marketing ploy for getting ups into Girolamar. I persuaded the kids to sit on the wall crying when couples were walking past. When decent people stopped to ask what was wrong, the little loves would sob that they were lost and that Mummy and Daddy were 'in there somewhere!' (pointing at Girolamar).

As the helpful couple escorted the wailing children into the complex, I would run round the back end of the building and meet them just before they got to the reception desk. I would nod understandingly whilst the good Samaritans explained the situation, but point out that this was a private club and they would need to check in as visitors. They would have to agree to be shown around for insurance purposes, but that this was just a bit of daft red tape, after which they could reunite the lost cherubs with their parents. While the couple were checking in, the kids pretended to want to go to the toilet, at which point we would disappear and head for the ice-cream bar. I would happily buy them the ice-creams of their choice as their well-earned reward.

Everyone was happy. I got my money, the kids got their cornets and the couple got introduced to an exciting new way of holidaymaking. That was the way I saw it anyway. The children's parents begged to differ. Apparently, when they discovered what was going on, they stormed into Carlos' office and objected vociferously. Their father had his hands around the throat of the American guy who owned the company, while their mother shrieked about going to the press. It took all the diplomacy of Girolamar's senior management to calm the situation down.

Fortunately for me it happened on my day off. Everyone had a chance to cool down before I turned up at work the next day. Oblivious to the previous day's events, I bounced into the morning meeting, expecting to clean up again with the help of my tiny accomplices.

Ben was already sipping his morning coffee when I arrived. He looked up, and from his expression I knew that I was in trouble.

'Morning Fagin,' he said. 'You're in the shit!'

'What's happened?' I wanted to know.

'Those kids that you were corrupting grassed you up and now their dad's going to kick your head in.'

'Is that all?'

'No, the owner of the company wants to fire you and keep all your wages. You have to go to his office right away.'

I wasn't really worried. Somehow I knew that I would be able to talk my way out of it. I did, but only by the skin of my teeth. After much huffing and puffing, Billy, the big gruff Texan guy who owned the company, fined me two hundred quid.

'This is your last warning, boy. You put one foot out of line from now on and I'll have every bone in your body broken!'

'I'll be careful,' I assured him, straight faced.

He eyed me with snarling scepticism.

'I never know when you English boys are taking the rise outta me,' he growled menacingly. 'Now go on, git!'

I went to tell Ben the verdict. We chatted for a bit and he told me that I was lucky to be fined only two hundred pounds.

'You're always in trouble with the companies you work for,' he told me.

He went quiet for a moment and stared.

'Who was it that chased you off Tenerife?' he asked.

'Pete and Alex. You know, the managers from Oasis,' I replied, not really wanting to go into it all.

'Do you mean that Pete over there?' said Ben curiously, pointing over my shoulder.

'No, no, no,' I sighed without looking round. 'Big Pete, the psycho from Darlington. The guy with the motorbike. He's in Tenerife.'

'I know who you mean, and he's over there.' Ben was still pointing.

I caught his expression and turned to look.

My heart stopped completely in my chest. There was Pete. Bigger than ever. He had seen us and was marching in my direction. He was about twenty feet away and, assuming my legs suddenly started working again, there was no way I could outrun him.

'You!' he thundered, raising one enormous arm to point at me.

He was wearing a pair of shorts and no t-shirt. His muscles were twitching furiously in the sun. He strode over and stood towering over me. Rage flashed in his eyes as he grabbed the front of my shirt. My mind was racing as I frantically tried to figure out some way of avoiding my impending fate.

'Erm, Pete, Hi . . . I can explain everything you know,' I gabbled as he backed me up against the wall. I could explain nothing. I had taken the piss and now I was going to pay. I fell silent and took a deep breath in readiness for the first blow.

It never came. I opened my eyes to find him and everyone else laughing.

'Gotcha there, didn't I?' he guffawed.

'You could say that, yes,' I confirmed.

The relief was enormous. I still couldn't quite believe that I was unharmed. Guardedly, I asked how he was doing. It turned out that he was fine and bore no grudge against me for my misbehaviour in The Grief. He and Alex had taken the line that Tom was to blame for leading me astray because he was a couple of years older. I told Pete that he had hit the nail on the head. It had taken me a while to see it, but at least I was rid of the bastard now!

Pete was over recruiting OPCs for Tenerife and wanted to take me and Ben out for a drink that night to discuss it.

'And Barry . . .'

'Yes?'

'Relax, pal. If I'd wanted to hurt you I would have done it already. You were too young to know any better, so we decided to let it slide. This time. Alex might want some money for the repair of his bike though.' He chuckled to himself and walked off.

I took Chris with me when I went for that drink with Pete and Ben. I was interested to see the offer on the table in case I wanted to go back to Tenerife.

Pete was on form throughout the evening. He was buying all the drinks. Very uncharacteristic behaviour for him as I found out in later years. He must have been badly in need of OPCs to be doing all this. I think this was the real reason why he was prepared to ignore my previous antics in Tenerife. In the end, Pete offered us free flights back over, accommodation and cars for one month. The usual deal. It was interesting because I preferred Tenerife to the mainland but I wanted to finish the season on the Costa before I went anywhere.

The next couple of weeks passed uneventfully in the usual blur of work, drink, drugs and sex. Then something strange happened. Chris disappeared.

I knew that he wasn't really enjoying the job but when he left it was still a bit sudden.

I was working my usual location one afternoon when he strolled casually up to me and asked if he could borrow my car. He wanted to go and do some shopping for that night's dinner. It didn't matter that he wasn't on the insurance, in Spain the police weren't bothered. I gave him the keys and he told me he would be back in twenty minutes.

An hour and a half later and he had still not returned and I was worried. I thought that he might have had an accident. I asked everyone around if they had seen him, and from their responses I worked out what had happened.

'Chris? He's driving back to England isn't he?'

'He said that you'd agreed to let him steal your hire car. Won't you get in trouble?'

I was a bit upset that he hadn't seen fit to inform me of his plans but I still gave him half a day's head start before I reported the theft. The car hire company wanted money from me. Something in the contract about having to pay the first five hundred pounds on a theft or accident claim. Luckily, I always made a point of lying about my address whenever I hired a vehicle. This meant that when they sent the police round to demand the money, I would be impossible to find.

As for Chris, he made it to England. Unluckily for him though, the girl who was travelling with him was caught smuggling a large package of marijuana through customs in her pants. Somehow he got dragged into the mess and, although he was actually innocent, he was held on remand, taken to court and was eventually fined over a grand.

Meanwhile, things were about to get awkward for me back on the Costa. I was just about to clock off and have a traditional Sunday lunch one weekend, at an English pub in Fuengirola, when I heard my name being shouted. I scanned the street in the direction of the noise to find Ben running towards me, frantically waving that day's copy of a very famous English newspaper.

'What have you done now?' he demanded. 'I can't believe you've been so stupid.'

## BLAGGERS

I stalled while I read the offending article. Deep down I already knew what had happened. The reporters had done a real hatchet job on timeshare and used Chris and I's names to back it up. We had been stitched up good and proper. Except, of course, that Chris had gone and therefore would not be bearing the brunt of the industry's anger. I had the feeling that that particular pleasure was going to be all mine.

I was right. It was a two-page article entitled 'Sex, Drugs and Timeshare'. Included was the photo of myself and Chris on the beach with the topless girls, looking as if we were saying 'fuck you' to the world in general. Throughout the article Chris and I revealed timeshare secrets, like how much we got paid and the lies we used to tell to get people to visit the complexes.

Fortunately, Ben was prepared to accept that I was the innocent victim of journalistic guile. There were others who wouldn't be so forgiving. Billy at Girolamar was livid and sent his security boys to find me. I would have been subjected to considerable violence had they caught up with me but, as with vehicle hire companies, I preferred not to tell my employers my correct address once I had moved out of company accommodation.

I basically had to go to ground for a week or so. Ben, who was the only person I trusted with the knowledge of my location, kept me informed of developments out in the world. All the OPCs on the Costa del Sol were outraged. There would have been plenty of motivation for any of the local ex-pat lunatics to be the one to find me and 'do the neccessaries'.

I had one thing in my favour. The photo in the paper was of such poor quality that I could not be readily identified among the tourists lying on the beach. So lie on the beach I did.

The season was coming to an end on the Costa. It is only busy on mainland Spain during the four or five months of summer. It seemed as good a time as any to head back to England, partly because of the low season and partly because it was no fun living incognito. The only worry I had about going home was facing my relatives. Dad was incensed about the article. He was convinced that the entire country had seen that specific edition of the paper and was blaming him alone.

'Tsk tsk, what a disgrace! Still, the lad's too young to know any better. It's quite obviously Chris's fault, the bastard.'

'Oh I totally agree. All down to Chris.'

The rest of the family were none too chuffed either – particulaly those bearing the same surname as myself, which was mentioned repeatedly in the article. Despite the impending lectures my mind was made up to do a 'prodigal'. I sunbathed like a man possessed for ten days or so, jumped on a plane, and returned home.

I got back to Yorkshire and spent a couple of days apologising to the more indignant members of my family. I was low on funds again and wondering what to do, when a cheque arrived for five hundred pounds. It was from the newspaper. Apparently it was a legal thing. If I accepted the cheque and cashed it, it was equivalent to saying that I stood by the story. Here was a moral dilemma. I could return the payment and claim outrage at such blatant misquotes, thereby regaining some of the credibility I had lost among my peers, or I could swallow my pride and take the money on the grounds that no-one ever wins in an argument with a newspaper.

I grabbed the money with both hands and bought myself a car. It was an old two-litre Cortina and I used it to hunt for a job. I told myself that at the ripe old age of twenty, it was time to grow up and settle down. To my disillusionment I found that jobs were hard to come by. This was England in a recession and I had no skills or trade.

In the end I got taken on as salesperson by a notorious vacuum cleaner company. I took to the work easily. We were selling these machines for over a thousand pounds each and, by comparison, even the cars in some of the punters' drives weren't worth that much. Not that this worried me. If they were prepared to buy, I was prepared to sell.

I finally left the job for two reasons. Firstly, my expenses were too high. It was one of those 'own car/own telephone' jobs and my outgoings ate heavily into my commission. Secondly, the excitement just wasn't there. Even when my colleagues asked me about my previous job, they sneered disbelievingly at my stories. That was yet another piece of wisdom I was to learn quite young:

no-one wants to hear of someone whose life is more interesting than their own, it only undermined them further.

I was dejected for a while but it made me realise that I had to go abroad and work again. I didn't want peace and stability. I wanted to take risks. I wanted to earn a lot and spend a lot. I wanted to be able to say, when I grew older, that I had lived life to the max! With this in mind I took a job in a local shop. I stayed until I got my first month's pay cheque which I used to finance my return to Tenerife. During that month I had time to plan my trip better than I had on previous occasions. I phoned a pal of mine who was working for a different company to Pete and Alex. This time I didn't want to be under their control. My friend's name was Jaffar and he was the manager of a French team for a company called Tropical Haven.

I rang him several times before flying over there. I made sure that my flight would be reimbursed as soon as I arrived and that I would have a large villa laid on as free accommodation. I also wanted to bring my buddy Alan with me, so I made sure he got the same deal.

Alan was a laid-back kind of a guy. He wanted to travel but wasn't really aggressive enough to do the timeshare. No problem, we thought, we'll find him work in the bars.

When the day came for us to leave, the familiar excitement took hold of me. A great weight lifted off my shoulders as I boarded the plane and, leaving behind the grey drudgery of the UK, I set off once more into the wide blue yonder.

# 6

# TENERIFE III

Jaffar picked us up from the airport and drove us to a spacious sea-view apartment. He could only speak French but I had learned a few languages by now and could translate for Alan. Owing to our poor financial situation, we decided to get cracking straightaway. Alan tried OPCing that afternoon but hated it, so that night we made our way down to the Veronica's strip to look for extra work. We took jobs as PRs in order to supplement our incomes. I blagged my way into my first-ever DJing job by claiming to have worked extensively in local radio in the UK. It was a just a small bar and I thought that it would be a doddle. After all, how hard could it be to stand in a DJ box and supply a bit of inane banter between records? The answer is bloody hard! It took less than ten minutes of scratched records, feedback and a non-dancing, hostile crowd before the bar manager rumbled me. He swiftly booted me back outside to PR with Alan, muttering in Spanish about me losing him business.

Our schedule was exhausting and we soon found it impossible to keep up both jobs. I stopped doing the bar touting at night so that I was fresher for the OPCing in the mornings. Alan went the other way and stopped doing the OPCing. Fair play to him, though, he was only in Tenerife to enjoy himself and he certainly did that. After a while our lifestyles took us in different directions. We remained friends but we saw each other very rarely after the first few weeks.

Meanwhile I was discovering the shortcomings of the company

I was working for. First of all it had no photo team. Therefore there was no opportunity to be promoted from the street. I didn't much fancy the prospect of slogging away all day under the sub-tropical sun for very long. Additionally, there was the fact that the club was owned by one of the notorious English gangsters that lived on the island. This guy ran his resort with the help of some particularly nasty clumpers and had a fearsome reputation for dealing harshly with members of his staff (or anybody else for that matter) who crossed him. The head clumper was away from Tenerife when I joined Tropical Haven. If he got back and noticed that I was working for him, I would never be able to leave the company. Bearing in mind that a couple of these blokes had killed a couple of angry Rottweilers in a straight fight for a bet, you can see why I was anxious to leave when I found out just who I was working for.

I was thinking about going back to Oasis Beach Club. Pete and Alex were no longer there, which was one good reason to rejoin. I wanted to work for a professional company, but one with no security, so Oasis was now my first choice for a transfer.

Oasis had had a difficult time getting rid of Pete. He had always let it be known that if any of the senior directors attempted to sack him, he would gouge their eyes out, which was probably the reason why Pete and Alex stayed for as long as they did.

Oasis was a small part of a multinational American concern and there had been worries at corporate levels about Pete and Alex's violent style of management for some time. They wanted to get rid of the big fellas and replace them with more traditional leadership. Pete knew this and when the Project Director finally summoned up the bottle to request a meeting to discuss it, Pete was well prepared. A few years later, when Pete and I were friends, he told me the story.

The PD of Oasis was called Cedric. He was American. Tall and dark, he was always immaculately attired in an expensive suit. He exuded style and confidence and, being a skilled negotiator, he arranged to have the meeting in his office. Presumably this was part of his strategy to gain some kind of psychological advantage by being on his own turf. This would normally be a good idea in a business situation but he had forgotten to take into account the very real element of physical danger to his person that was involved in this instance. When Pete and Alex came in and shut the door, which was the only exit bar a two-storey window, Cedric suddenly found that he was actually in a bit of a lobster pot. He had no choice but to go ahead with what they all knew they were there for, which was to work out a golden handshake that would enable Oasis to continue its operation unhindered by the threat of harm to its workforce.

Cedric now had the distinct disadvantage of knowing that there was a good chance he would take a swan-dive out of the window if they couldn't agree on a suitable pay-off figure.

Pete could see the fear in Cedric's eyes and decided to capitalise.

'Fifty grand!' he barked, his gaze locked on the smaller man.

Cedric did not seem shocked by the size of the sum and seemed about to agree. The big fellas glanced at each other in surprise.

'Each!' growled Alex quickly.

Cedric still seemed unruffled and made another attempt to close the deal.

'I can live with tha . . .' he began.

'And a grand a week each for life!' interrupted Pete, testing the water still further.

Cedric's mouth finally dropped open.

'What? . . . You mean forever?' he spluttered. Clearly this was way beyond his brief.

'Alright then, for nine months,' said Pete decisively.

And the deal was struck! They would receive their money in the form of a cheque for fifty thousand pounds each straightaway. A contract was signed stating that Alex and Pete were to stay out of Spain and the Canary Islands for nine months. Another stipulation was that they didn't have anything to do with the business of timeshare during this period. In return for their compliance, Pete and Alex would also receive a cheque for a thousand pounds each per week during the time of their absence.

The relevance of this little episode to me was that with the big fellas gone, there was now no reason why I should not go back and work for Oasis.

I went for a drink with Jenny, a friend of mine who was a manager at Oasis. She was the person who did my training course when I first started in timeshare back in1988. As well as the free month's accommodation, she offered me rapid promotion to the photo team if I proved myself on the street to Wubbo, the new marketing manager.

I made the transition back to Oasis quite easily. Once again I was surrounded by friendly young people. My accommodation was shared with kids who were brand new to the business, so, because of my experience, I was revered as some kind of timeshare guru which suited me nicely. I took a week's holiday before I started working again in order to get to know my new colleagues better. Then it was time to knuckle down to it. I had to prove myself, not just to Wubbo, but also to the OPCs who had learned all about me. Wubbo had interviewed me before taking me on and he had told me that I would have to do extremely well on the street before he could promote me. He also gave me a personal 'spif' (Special Performance Incentive Fund – a spif was a bonus offered as a reward for good work). My spif was one hundred pounds on top of my wages if I got three couples on my first day. I got four, impressing everyone from the other OPCs to Jenny and Wubbo, who started me on the photo team that very week.

Although most of the people working at the company were strangers to me, some of the old crowd were still there, including a pal of mine called Brandon. He had been Pete's personal assistant but under the Wubbo administration he had risen to become a street captain in his own right. Tom and I had shared a villa with him when I moved out of my first-ever company accommodation. It had been a scary house to live in because all three of us were constantly trying to photograph each other in the nude. I hasten to add that this was not motivated by any kind of homosexual inclination, rather, every winter, timeshare companies in the Canaries recruit batches of Scandinavian OPCs in an effort to fleece the Norwegian, Danish, Swedish and Finnish tourists, who frequent the islands at this time of year. The blond-haired, blue-eyed Scandi OPCs were eagerly awaited by the rest of us. Including

Pete and Alex. They were such big fans of Scandinavian women that during Scandi season they put on a standing spif of ten pounds, payable to anyone who furnished them with photographs of naked OPCs. This sparked off a frenzy of amateur photography but, predictably enough, all the photos were obtained by lads bursting in on each other while in the shower or halfway through a dump. Very few of the snapshots were of the girls, who took extreme precautions not to be captured on celluloid.

Tom, Brandon and I made a pact not to get involved in these childish games and foolishly I took them at their word. We were sharing a one-bedroom gaff at the time and, having drawn the short straw, I was the one who slept on the couch.

Late one night, believing the others to be asleep, I was settling down to a quick one-handed drum solo, as young lads are wont to do from time to time. As I was working my way towards the inevitable I was distracted by some faint rustling noises from the kitchen. I stopped for a moment and listened, but everything had gone quiet. Ah well, probably just the wind, I naïvely concluded as I settled back into my rhythm. Wait! Was that a door creaking? Again I ceased all activity and concentrated, trying to discern whether or not the sound was real or just my paranoia. Nothing but silence. I decided to stop letting my imagination run away with me and get on with the job in hand (so to speak!). As soon as I reached the point of no return, disaster struck. With a triumphant roar Tom and Brandon burst into the living-room with their cameras flashing frantically. The sheets were ripped away from me as the lights came on and the cameras were thrown from one to the other as I played a berserk game of piggy-in-the-middle.

When I had calmed down, given up and had a shower, it was time to negotiate. I eyed up Tom and Brandon.

'I suppose you want the tenner that you would have got for the spif?' I offered, attempting to sound casual.

'Oh no, Barry, it's not that easy,' smiled Tom. 'We want to give these to Pete at the morning meeting for a laugh.'

The blood drained from my face as the picture formed in my mind.

'All right, how much?' I squeaked, my throat constricting with fear.

Tom and Brandon were grinning broadly by now.

'Well, we took eight photos at ten pounds each . . .' began Brandon.

'You robbing bastards!' I gasped.

'. . . so that'll be one hundred pounds!' summed up Tom.

'Eh? But eight times ten is only . . .' I trailed off.

'Hmm?' they smiled in unison. The look on their faces told me that logic was going to play no part in this discussion. I paid up grudgingly, muttering under my breath about how the slimy gits were going to get it back in spades (and they did, but that's another story). The point of this is merely to illustrate that although I was glad to see Brandon again, I was happy not to be sharing with him and Tom anymore.

Also around were Jo and Ron. Events had taken their inevitable course and Ron was showing his true colours as a bully. They had bought a converted bus and were living at a camp site. Another joint acquisition was Pete's motorbike when he left the island. I suspect that it was Ron's idea for them to buy this, as Jo was unable to ride it. Ron fluctuated between worshipping Jo and beating her up. I was really pleased to see Jo again but the first time I saw Ron, he explained quite clearly that I better not cross him or I knew what the consequences would be.

I took the hint. I saw Jo when I could but it was uncomfortable being in Ron's constant presence.

Also still around was a smooth Belgian guy of about 40 by the name of Henk. He was the best OPC on the photo team and was living with a beautiful French girl who was Princess Stephanie of Monaco's first cousin. Henk was a good friend of mine and later we would do a spot of travelling together.

I teamed up for the photo team with Kate, a cheeky little cockney girl who was a good friend of Jo, and an excellent photo OPC. The first night we worked together we were blessed with success. I blagged the couples for all I was worth. I changed people's ages to fit the qualifications (the ups had to be between 25 and 65 years old for the OPC to get paid) and tricked them into visiting Oasis by any means necessary.

We put five couples in. I took advantage of the fact that the salespeople didn't know me very well in order to get away with some particularly ruthless blags before they had a chance to learn how to catch me out. We got all five paid on. The rest of the photo team only had three between them, so we looked like superstars.

It was the beginning of a golden period for me at work. I was buzzing from all the attention I was getting for being a top OPC again and this, in turn, kept me in high spirits for work.

In Tom's absence I moved in with Brandon, who, despite being a Brummie, is an extremely likeable chap. Ten years older than me, he was a keen body-builder of about 5ft 7in. He wore glasses and had dark hair cut in a severe flat top. Brandon possessed a ready wit and somehow his comments seemed funnier because of his broad Brummie accent. Our villa was in Los Christianos, which is a bit quieter than Las Americas and also meant that we got a better deal rent-wise.

Brandon and I became unofficial entertainment managers for the company. Every Saturday night there was a party for all the Oasis workers. The firm put a few hundred quid behind the bar at a club in the Veronicas at which the Brandster and myself would compère. We used to get on the mike and organise daft games for the evening. By doing this we ensured that we were always the centre of attention, which gave us a big advantage in the ongoing competition to seduce the new female OPCs and the salesgirls. In the face of such obvious sexism, I should add that the competition among our female colleagues was just as fierce when it came to unsuspecting new lads joining the Oasis family. In the daytime Brandon and I would cruise around in one of our cars, overseeing his OPCs and scoping out any new talent. It was a thoroughly enjoyable existence and we soon acquired another good friend whose nickname was Toronto, because that was where he came from. He became part of our crew and, between the three of us, we were gradually working our way into the partying history books.

It was around this time that I first got introduced to cocaine, which was to become a regular expense and a severe obstacle to saving money. Cocaine Hydrochloride is the chemical equivalent of sticking the nozzle of a powerful vacuum cleaner into your wallet every time you go out – it sucked the wages from mine for years.

My first dalliance was when Kate and I were worried about losing a competition at work. The prize was an all-expenses-paid trip to anywhere in the USA with a grand each spending money. This competition had been put on by my friend Henk, who had recently been promoted to photo team captain.

Kate and I were in the lead but it was a close call. Jo and Ron looked like they were going to catch us up. I had never taken coke before but had heard that it gave you unlimited energy as well as a confidence boost. I asked Kate if she thought that taking some at work would increase the chances of us winning the America trip. She said that she was game to try it if I was.

We approached Luis, the Spanish guy who owned the photo studio that our company dealt with, because we knew that he sold coke as a sideline. He was our friend, so we thought that he'd give us a good deal on the stuff.

Luis seemed strangely disappointed when we asked him (strange because he was, after all, a drug dealer!). He agreed to sell us a gram of Charlie and, on the last day of the competition, Kate and I snorted several lines each, before, during and after work. While it didn't get us any more ups, it did make us babble like loons at the unfortunate couples who happened to be in our bars that night. Although we felt like we were on top of the world and were overflowing with witty, interesting conversation, the reality was somewhat different. All we did was exhibit the classic symptoms of people on cocaine: talking too much, being hyperactive and not listening to anyone else when they tried to get a word in edgeways. Consequently, we got no bookings and finished second in the competition. We won a very nice camera but missed out on the America trip. You might think that this incident would have put me off the idea of using Charlie, but no! During the next nine years or so I wasted untold hard-earned cash on the stuff. But hey! When we party, we party hearty!

## BLAGGERS

My pal Toronto was the company jester. Very tall, slim and good-looking, he was travelling for a few years before he joined the Canadian Air Force. He was of Italian descent but north European in appearance. An amiable chap, he was liked by everybody. The girls loved him for his good looks and easy-going nature. The lads enjoyed his company because he was a renowned party animal. He was one of those people who is terminally skint, yet always seems to have money for drinking or buying clothes. He was regularly getting into scrapes of one kind or another but possessed an alarming ability to escape without consequence, mostly due to the fact that everyone had a soft spot for him.

One such occasion springs to mind when Jeff, a company director, was visiting from America. Jeff was only 24 and his father was golfing buddies with the owner of the American conglomerate that owned Oasis. This wasn't the sole reason for his elevated status, however, Jeff was also a graduate of Harvard Business School and had proved himself many times over on the corporate battlefield. Part of his job was to ensure the continued success of Oasis. In order to perform this function effectively, he used to fly into Tenerife at least once a month and stick his nose into everybody's business. His usual course of action was to go to one random meeting for each department and, when he did, it was best behaviour all round for everyone else. Jeff would tolerate neither poor performance nor waste. After going over the figures, he would dish out praise or punishment as he saw fit.

One night it was the turn of the photo team to have their monthly performance meeting with Jeff. We filed into the room silently, hoping, as we did on these occasions, that we hadn't done anything too seriously wrong. If he was pleased with us, it was even possible that we might get a special competition or spif put on. We were only told that it was going to be Jeff who was taking the meeting ten minutes beforehand – mainly because he liked to see how punctual we were, how smartly we dressed for work etc. Obviously, everyone would make a special effort if we had advance warning of the 'raid'.

We sat around the large table in the meeting room. As usual, the films, camera batteries and previous night's photos were stacked at the head of the table ready for distribution by our team captain, Henk.

Jeff also took up position at the head of the table and, after the customary individual greeting to show that he cared on a personal level, he got the meeting under way. He was extremely concerned, it turned out, about the enormous costs of the photo team. We were supposed to average 20 photographs for each couple that we took to the resort. Understandably, we couldn't persuade all the photo recipients to visit the timeshare the next day. Some photos were of couples who had already been. Sometimes we would have to take free photos of the waiters to keep them sweet. The photos were expensive and Jeff was angry because he was sure that we were being too free and easy with them. He was in the middle of giving us all a stern talk about waste, when out of the corner of my eye I noticed that Toronto was looking worried and shifting uneasily in his seat. Curious, I began watching him more closely. He started rocking his chair back and forth. Yup, he was definitely anxious about something.

Jeff was thundering away, demanding to know why we were taking three times as many photos as we should be. The reason for this was obvious to all the OPCs: we used the company film and cameras to take photos on nights out, or days at the beach. We considered this to be an unofficial perk of the job and we also used to hand the films in with our work photos for the company to develop.

When you dropped your films into the studio's letter-box at the end of a night's work, you identified them as yours by writing your marketing number on them. For example, Kate and I's number was PH007. The next night the studio delivered all the photos to the office in separate envelopes, one envelope per team. The one with your number on it would contain your previous night's photos.

Jeff informed us that in order to highlight what he meant about waste, he was going to pick a couple of teams at random and go through their photographs. He was going to make clear the distinction between that which was necessary and that which was waste, by fining the OPCs a tenner for every frivolous photo that he found in their envelope. I knew that on this particular occasion I had handed in no private photos, so I was quite relaxed and ready to enjoy the show.

By way of contrast, Toronto seemed to be having difficulty breathing. I watched in amusement as he leaned back and surreptitiously stood up. His chair was quickly nabbed by one of the OPCs who had arrived too late to get one.

Jeff had chosen Ron and Jo's photos and was talking his way through them. He fined the pair of them for three personal snaps but seemed disappointed at not having chosen a more wasteful example.

Toronto meanwhile was covertly manoeuvring through the groups of standing OPCs, towards the rest of the photos. Jeff was standing right over them, one hand resting on the pile as he talked. Toronto edged right up to the side of the table next to them.

I was intrigued. Toronto was obviously going to try and whip his photos out of the pile but I couldn't see how he was going to manage it without Jeff noticing. All the while, the rest of the team remained unaware of the little drama that was unfolding.

It appeared as though Toronto hadn't breathed during the whole operation and now his attention was entirely focused on his envelope. Judging his moment precisely, when Jeff was looking in the opposite direction, Toronto's hand darted out towards the pile.

Unfortunately, Jeff turned back round at exactly the wrong moment. Luckily for Toronto, Jeff interpreted the outstretched hand as an invitation for a handshake. Perplexed, he complied.

'Hey Toronto, how're ya doin'?' he asked in his New England nasal twang.

'Yeah, great!' came Toronto's strangled reply. His forced grin fooled no-one.

'Let's have a look at your photos then,' said Jeff light-heartedly, reaching for them.

'No, no, let's not bother, I'm in a hurry to get to work.' Toronto attempted to swerve the request as he swiftly grabbed the envelope.

'Seriously Toronto, I want to see those photos.' Jeff's amiable tone now carried a warning note.

'No!' snapped Toronto, probably a lot louder than he meant to. He gulped and tried to look casual.

'What's the problem, John?' (Toronto's real name). Jeff grabbed for the photos and caught Toronto by surprise. Horror registered in the Canadian's features.

'There might be a couple of photos of some dogs in there,' he muttered hurriedly. He glanced around at the team then back at Jeff, self-consciously wiping his hand across his nose. He looked like a rabbit caught in car headlights.

All the while, Jeff's expression was going through some fascinating changes. From shock to disgust to naked anger as he checked through the envelope. He turned slowly to lock eyes with the terrified Toronto as he started flipping the photos, one at a time, onto the table. I grinningly craned to have a look. There were two entire films taken of a couple of dogs making 'the beast with two heads' on the street outside one of the restaurants Toronto worked. Jeff's face was purple with anger. While he was trying to articulate his fury, Toronto mouthed the words, fuck this! and fled the room in panic.

This didn't serve to placate Jeff in the slightest and his head whipped back round towards the rest of us. We looked down at our feet, valiantly resisting the urge to crumple with laughter. It was like that scene in Monty Python's *Life of Brian* where the legionnaires are holding back their laughter to avoid the wrath of Michael Palin's Caesar.

'Who thinks this is funny?' raged Jeff.

Thirty photo OPCs struggled desperately to hold their mirth. Everybody concentrated on avoiding eye contact with Jeff, knowing that to meet his gaze would be to lose control entirely. In the ensuing silence the pressure to laugh intensified. Kate cracked and her screeching guffaws were the catalyst that released the rest of our violent convulsions. Tears were streaming down people's faces as they gave vent to the pressure within.

Jeff ranted and railed for us to stop and take it seriously. He had no hope. We only stopped when he had left the room in defeat.

'Oh dear!' said Kate when she had calmed down.

'We're in trouble now!' agreed Henk.

And we were. Jeff fined us one hundred pounds each. Toronto was sacked but got reinstated two days later, thus not suffering in the least. He even avoided paying a fine because his punishment had been the sacking. No-one held it against him though. It was the kind of thing expected of him and life would certainly have been a lot duller without him around.

The year rolled on. Tenerife's version of winter is quite a bit hotter than even the balmiest English summer. We were eagerly waiting to cash in on Scandi season. Because timeshare was relatively new in the Viking lands, the media up there hadn't yet begun warning people about OPCs and couples from Scandinavia were therefore notoriously easier to trick than their less blond counterparts.

We were also awaiting the arrival of the Scandi OPCs. I've always found the Scandi lads a good laugh and partying traditionally stepped up a level when they came to the island. Of course, there was a more basic reason as to why the male OPCs were so keen for the Scandis to arrive: Scandinavian girls weren't only beautiful, but also displayed a very liberal attitude towards sex. Yahoo! The female Brits on our team thoroughly resented them. During Scandi season they would stomp around muttering things like, 'Those Scandis are so plastic looking, they look like Barbi dolls,' and, 'We British girls are so much more down to earth, don't you think?'

We lads would go, 'Yeah, yeah, whatever!' without our gazes leaving whichever blonde goddess happened to be wiggling past at the time.

Usually my flings with Scandi lasses were pleasantly pointless. I regarded them, as I'm sure they regarded me, as a bit of harmless fun. In fact, up until this point in my life, I had never taken any relationship too seriously. I thought love, in the words of the Monkees, was only true in fairytales. All that was about to change.

I was driving down the strip one morning with Toronto, music blasting out of the speakers, eyeing up the girls on the way to the beach, when it happened. I noticed a pal of ours working with what was obviously a new OPC. I could only see her from behind but what I saw was sufficiently interesting for me to slow down for a better look. She turned round in slow motion. When our eyes met I was mesmerised. Her beauty incapacitated me like a well-aimed kick in the groin – the hint of a smile, huge dark eyes and black hair down to the small of her back. I was spellbound.

I became aware of Toronto shouting at me. Gradually I came round from the trance I was in.

'What is it?' I asked him, irritated at being torn away from this vision of femininity.

'You're going to smash into that car!' he informed me.

'Eh?'

SMASH!

The car in front had stopped and I had ploughed right into it. Red as a beetroot, I quickly looked around at the girl and yes, she had seen it.

'Are you guys OK?' she asked, genuinely concerned. I felt such an idiot. I tried to regain some measure of dignity by thinking of something clever to say but as soon as I looked at her the intensity of my attraction overwhelmed me.

'Glarg, ng flrr thnnth,' I managed to mutter before my attention was drawn away by the irate taxi driver whose vehicle I had crashed into. He insisted on talking English and so, with this girl standing next to me, I was forced to explain that I had been looking at her when I should have been watching the road. The taxi driver was in his mid-50s and quite conservative looking. The expression on his face made clear what he thought of little foreign twerps like myself being allowed to drive on his island. He walked back to his vehicle shaking his head in disgust.

Despite this somewhat unfortunate start I didn't give up. I had to find out more about the incredible creature by my side. The problem was that her presence still seemed to have a direct effect upon my ability to articulate.

'Want go out, me, you, together!' I babbled. 'Tonight?'

Amazingly she smiled and nodded. Her name was Ira and she was from Sweden. After chatting for a few minutes, I found out that she had just started with Oasis. She was about 5ft 10in., twenty-two years old and wearing strange clothes. I can't remember her exact attire, but throughout the time I knew her, nonconformity to the world of fashion was to be one of her trademarks. That is not to say that she looked like an oddball – just that, as in all aspects of her life, she didn't seem shackled by the conventions that keep the rest of us in check.

After we finished work on the photo team that evening, Toronto and I met up with her and a friend of hers, whose name was Anna. We took them to a bar called Strikers. This was a pleasantly bohemian watering-hole and a favourite of Toronto's and mine. They played a lot of old Rolling Stones, Kinks and Bob Dylan tracks and they always had a couple of members of staff on lookout at the door in case the police showed up, enabling the customers inside to take drugs in peace. If the two PRs on sentry duty came running back into the bar, everyone would go into a frenzy of swallowing and snorting.

It was a good choice of venue because the two girls loved the place. We got to know them over a few spliffs. Ira and Anna turned out to be on the same wavelength as us and as the night wore on I found myself more and more fascinated by Ira. Circumstance worked against me in that I was sitting next to Anna and ended up talking mainly to her while Toronto chatted with Ira. There was no sociable way to turn this around, so, apart from stolen glances, my contact with Ira was minimal and I became engrossed instead with her friend. Anna was a lovely girl and great company but unable to command my full attention in the light of her companion.

Around five o'clock in the morning I dropped the other three off at company accommodation and went home. Normally I would have made a play for Anna but on this occasion I was too struck by Ira to accept anything less.

The next morning I met up with Toronto for breakfast as usual. Predictably he had slept with Ira and I was gutted. I made light of it and Toronto was totally unaware of the impact that Ira had made on me. He was only shocked by my not sleeping with Anna, whom he had thought was the prettier of the two,

'She was begging for it, man,' he noted in his usual politically correct manner.

'Probably,' I grunted disinterestedly and changed the subject. There was no way I was going to admit to anything as soft as getting wound up over a girl.

I next saw Ira and Anna when I was dropping off some new OPCs in a small town called Paraiso. They were as friendly as ever and we went drinking at a little beach bar for the afternoon. Privately I forgave Ira for sleeping with Toronto that previous night. My feelings for her were so powerful that I deliberately held back. I knew that the closer I got, the greater the potential for pain.

Over the next few weeks and months, Ira and I developed a strong bond. We both, however, slept with other people. I made a special effort to be more sexually active than usual in a vain attempt to delay the inevitable. We had kissed a few times when we were out drinking and she probably wondered what I was playing at. There was some kind of sixth sense telling me not to get involved, but all the time I was falling deeper and deeper in love with her.

One night I stayed at her house because I wasn't capable of driving home. We slept in her bed and were kissing passionately. We couldn't have gone any further anyway because of Ira's annoying flatmate, Catrina: a 40-year old Norwegian woman who slept on the couch. The apartment was a studio, so we would have woken her had we made any noise.

Ira whispered to me that she found it strange that we had never made love together.

'Yeah, still, there's always tomorrow when your flatmate goes on holiday,' I yawned hopefully, as I drifted off to sleep.

The next night we went out as usual. Tension was in the air as we drove back to her flat. We went in. Wordlessly we kissed, undressing each other. I laid her down on the bed and gently kissed her stomach. I trailed my tongue downwards, gauging my performance from her whispered pleas. She gripped her hands behind my neck then pulled my head up towards hers. I entered her effortlessly. The decision to abandon myself had been made. Then we heard the key in the door.

We looked at each other and froze. Catrina was back. We quickly pulled the sheets up over us as she bustled into the apartment. She turned the lights on and headed for the fridge, complaining that her flight had been delayed by twelve hours. Dropping her cases on the floor, she grabbed a Coke and turned towards us.

'Oh, hello Barry, I didn't notice you there, not disturbing you two am I?'

Ira and I exchanged glances and burst into giggles.

'No, you're all right,' we told her. 'Make us a coffee and tell us about it.'

The atmosphere had gone. When we finished talking, Ira and I fell asleep in each other's arms.

Neither of us mentioned anything about the incident the next day and during the following week I backed off again. Toronto was sharing a flat with an Irish girl called Maria. A few days later I spent the night with her and when I got up in the morning I met Ira on the way to the bathroom. Unaware that I had been there she had gone home with Toronto. We swapped embarrassed greetings and passed each other by.

Life on the island was about to go through some major changes. Brandon rushed up to me one morning with disturbing news: Pete and Alex were back and were more than likely going to cause trouble. Their nine months of contractual absence was up and, far from using the time to pursue other directions in life, they had plans to profit once again from the Tenerife timeshare scene. I saw them later that day. They had obviously been hitting the steroids heavily as they were now even more formidable and powerful looking than before. Even their motorbikes were bigger. Alex had an enormous Goldwing and Pete had a black Kawasaki racing bike. They had also brought nine or ten fearsome-looking clumpers with them. The moment I saw them milling around the entrance to Oasis, I knew that things weren't going to run smoothly for the company.

## BLAGGERS

The rumour was that they were going to close Oasis down unless they were paid a hefty protection fee. You might wonder how this would be possible in a modern European country. Well, most of the timeshare executives were working illegally, yet others were on the run from the police in their home countries, so none of them had the option of asking the local law for help in this situation. In any case, they were all too scared of Pete and his crew to risk being caught 'grassing' on him.

None of us OPCs got any work done for the next couple of days. Our managers were busy telling us that everything was fine and not to worry but I was doubtful. I thought I would wait until Oasis had come to some kind of arrangement with Pete, rather than risk doing work that I might not get paid for. I felt certain that either Oasis or the big fellas would make a move soon.

Sure enough, four days later, Pete put the word about that there was going to be a meeting in a reclusive bar for all the OPCs and salespeople from Oasis – attendance was compulsory, if you knew what was good for you.

The anxiety was almost palpable among the throng of illegal workers gathered at the El Mirador bar. Pete and his lads were there long before everyone else but they made us wait while they had a little conference outside. When they eventually came in they all stood at the front of the bar. An expectant hush fell over the crowd. Pete looked over the audience silently before beginning his speech.

'Most of you know who I am,' he said in a businesslike tone. 'Those of you who don't can come to the front and find out if you like.' There were no takers. 'My name is Pete. I'm going to be closing Oasis down for a time while we negotiate some financial matters. None of you may go to work until further notice. My colleagues here will be driving around town for the next couple of days dishing out beatings to anyone they catch disobeying me. Does anybody have a problem with that?'

We all shuffled our feet and looked at the ceiling. The general consensus echoing around the room was that it seemed fair enough to us. In other words, bollocks to being the first person to stick his neck out and complain.

'Good. Off you all pop then,' he said, turning towards the bar. A thought struck him. 'Wait, I want to see the following people in private.' He reeled off a list of names. They were all good OPCs and salespeople. My own name was included. Everyone not on the list filtered out. Curious glances were cast back at the chosen few who were gathering round Pete at the bar. I gathered with the rest of them. I wondered what would happen now but I didn't really want to hang around any longer than necessary. I knew better than to want to be in the vicinity of Pete when he was making a power-play. I happened to know something about how he had achieved it in the past.

When Pete had originally managed to get himself and Alex promoted to marketing managers at Oasis, it had been through a combination of cunning and downright nastiness.

Although the two of them had already been street captains and were earning a nice little income, the next step up the ladder was the big one. As street captains they would have earned about five hundred pounds a week each. A marketing manager back then was on about a grand a week. The trouble being that there was only one marketing manager's position in each company. Their then current manager, Lee, was quite happy where he was, and as he was doing a good job, there was little hope of the big fellas replacing him – that was until Pete decided to engineer Lee's breakdown. How? You might well ask. It happened like this.

Jeff was keeping a far tighter rein on the company at that time and was permanently based in Tenerife. Pete began putting rumours about that Lee was going mad and the word filtered back to Jeff. He asked Pete and Alex to find out if there was any truth to the matter. He said that although he himself hadn't seen any evidence of it, he would hate to think that one of his staff might be having a breakdown without his knowledge.

Pete hummed and hawed and tried to avoid answering. Finally, he hung his head and said that although he hated to be a grass, yes, Lee was behaving a bit strangely at that moment.

'Strange? In what way?' Jeff wanted to know.

'Well, he's stomping around muttering to himself quite a lot,' said Pete.

'And staring at people,' chipped in Alex. 'Those cold piercing eyes . . .'

'Really?' asked Jeff, concerned.

'Seems to think that the company's got it in for him,' continued Pete. 'Mentions you quite a lot actually.'

Jeff snapped out of it.

'Rubbish!' he affirmed. 'Tell him I want to see him tonight in the marketing office. We'll soon see who's mad around here.'

'You did ask,' Alex told him with a sigh. 'We'll tell him you want to see him.'

That evening Pete and Alex 'accidentally' bumped into Lee and insisted on him coming for a drink to celebrate Pete's birthday. Pete went to the bar and when he came back with the beers he slipped a pipette full of liquid into Lee's bottle. The liquid was the boiled-up juice of ten 'trips' of LSD, or, in layman's terms, one bloody enormous dose.

'Your good health, sir,' he said jovially, as they toasted one another's future.

An hour later, they had finished their drink and Alex mentioned, as though he had forgotten, that Jeff wanted to see Lee in the marketing office.

'I think it's a set-up Lee,' confided Pete seriously. 'I think he wants to kill you.'

'What?' spluttered Lee. 'What did you say?'

'Nothing,' said Pete, puzzled. 'I didn't say anything. Are you OK Lee? You look a bit peaky.'

'You said something about Jeff wanting to kill me,' stated Lee. 'I heard you.'

'Jeff wants to kill you? Are you sure?' asked Pete curiously. 'Mind you, it would explain a few things. Still, not kill you, surely?'

'No, no, you said it,' said Lee bewildered. The LSD was beginning to take effect.

'Kill you, kill you, Jeff wants to kill you,' said Alex under his breath while Lee was looking at Pete. When Lee's head whipped back round, Alex's innocent smile was back in place.

'Lee, I think you'd better go and lie down after your meeting with Jeff. Pete's right, you are definitely looking under the weather.'

'Take care of him first,' Pete whispered viciously. 'Get him before he gets you!'

'Come on, Pete, we'd best be off,' continued Alex, as though Pete had said nothing. 'Don't forget your meeting with Jeff, Lee!'

And with that they sauntered off, leaving Lee totally confused at the bar. As soon as they were out of sight, round the corner, Pete and Alex sprinted over to the marketing office, to find Jeff waiting for his appointment with Lee.

'Jeff, thank God we got here in time!' gasped Pete. 'Lee is telling everyone that he is after you. Let me and Alex stay here to make sure you're OK.'

Jeff looked disbelieving. He thought about it for a moment. Then cowardice got the better of him.

'All right, you guys stay here, but don't say a word. I'll make my own mind up. Have you got that?'

'Oh yes, Jeff. As long as we know that you're safe. You won't even notice we're here,' Alex assured him.

Lurching footsteps were heard in the corridor. A rapping sound at the door. In came Lee. His eyes were wild and staring. His clothes dishevelled.

'You!' he growled at Jeff. 'I oughta kill you right now!'

'Jesus,' gulped Jeff. 'What's the matter, Lee?'

'Don't give me that, Jeff. I know you want me dead!'

'What are you talking about, Lee?' asked Pete, shocked. 'Jeff is your friend. We all are.'

'Er, yes, that's right,' confirmed Jeff, who had been thrown off balance by Lee's outburst. He pulled himself together and attempted to take control of the conversation.

'Now get a hold of yourself Lee and tell me exactly what's wrong.'

He did say it commandingly and Lee might well have calmed down. Except for the fact that behind Jeff's back Pete was staring at Lee, mouthing the words 'kill him, kill him now'. Then he started drawing his finger across his throat and pointing at Jeff.

Alex was also out of Jeff's range of vision and was motioning for Lee to grab one of the pens from the table and stab Jeff in the neck with it.

Lee lunged for the pen. He was so quick that he nearly got to Jeff before Pete and Alex wrestled him to the floor. Jeff's face went white.

'Get him out of here,' he shrieked. 'He's a fucking lunatic!'

'Now calm down, Jeff,' Pete implored. 'He's not mad, just ill. He needs help that's all. Here, you go home and we'll take him to hospital.'

Jeff was unconvinced and would go nowhere near him.

'Right. Whatever you say. Just get him out of *here*!'

They took Lee out to the car park and ushered him into the back of Alex's car. Pete got in next to him. They drove poor Lee into the wilderness, miles from town. Then they dragged him out of the car. Alex told Lee sternly that the best thing to do would be to approach Jeff's house 'cross-country' and kill him in the night. Then the police wouldn't catch him on the way.

They left him to make his way across the volcanic landscape by moonlight as they drove, laughing, to Jeff's villa.

Their amusement had been replaced with expressions of concern by the time they knocked on Jeff's door.

'He's escaped, Jeff. We opened the door to let him out at the hospital and he ran screaming into the night,' Pete informed him.

'Yes, something about murdering you if it was the last thing he ever did,' agreed Alex. 'I couldn't really hear him properly.'

'So maybe we had better stay here tonight to protect you,' suggested Pete.

Jeff agreed shakily. They were all stepping inside when Pete suddenly realised,

'Jeff!' he cried. 'Who's going to run the marketing department tomorrow? Lee is in no fit state to handle it.'

'Will you two take over his role?' asked Jeff without blinking. 'I think you're ready and besides, I owe you for tonight.'

Pete and Alex had to think about it. After all, it was a lot of responsibility and look what the pressure had done to Lee. Jeff convinced them to give it a try at least, by offering them a grand a week each.

Lee was arrested trying to break into Jeff's house later on that night and deported back to England for medical treatment.

So that's how Pete and Alex were promoted to marketing managers at Oasis, where I first met them. Hence my caution when they told all the good OPCs and salespeople to stay behind after that meeting at El Mirador.

I was right to be concerned. As soon as everyone else had gone, Pete told us that as part of his campaign to extort money from Oasis, he was going to have to tax its most successful employees – five grand each, to be exact. It was completely unavoidable, apparently, and if there had been any other way of doing it, he would have, of course, reconsidered. But there it was! Had to be done – so who was going to pay straightaway as opposed to instalments? He sounded so reasonable that some of the newer OPCs were actually standing there discussing the relative merits of paying one hundred pounds a week instead of just getting it out of the way in one go.

I was choking. I didn't have five grand, and bollocks to Pete's 'easy pay' system. I dropped below his line of sight behind a group of people. On my hands and knees, I shuffled quietly towards the door.

'Stay where you are, Barry,' said Pete casually, without looking up. 'I take it you want to pay by instalments?'

'Yes, Pete. You read my mind,' I replied, standing up foolishly.

'OK then, let's say two hundred pounds a week. I'll let you know when your first payment is due. Bye then.'

'Eh?'

'Well, you were trying to sneak off, weren't you?'

I trudged out of the bar. Cursing quietly, I waited in front of the bar entrance for the other OPCs. We all chewed the matter over in the car park. Everyone else had accepted the necessity of paying. I wasn't going to argue with them but my mind was already made up to try and weasel my way out of it.

I caught sight of Ira, who was waiting for me to drive her back to town. As I was chatting to her by the car I heard Pete's voice booming out of the entrance to the bar.

'Barry! Come here, I want to talk to you!' he announced in his usual forthright manner. I could see Ira looking at him with interest and I decided to try and keep them apart.

'Stay here for a minute, Ira,' I told her. 'I'm just going for a chat with Pete. Back in a sec.' Leaving her by the car, I strode off to see what he wanted.

'Anything wrong?' I asked chirpily.

Pete wasn't listening.

'Who's that?' he demanded, staring over my shoulder and pointing at Ira.

'Who? Who are you looking at? I can't see anyone,' I replied, studiously ignoring the fact that there was no-one else in her section of the car park.

'Her, there, standing by your car. Long black hair down to her arse. Bring her to me at once!'

His tone brooked no argument. If I hadn't complied, he would only have walked over to her anyway. In his current mood I didn't feel that it would be wise to wind him up any further. I went back over to Ira.

'What does Pete want?' she asked. I could see curiosity in her eyes. I knew that she had a track record of being attracted to psychotic men and would therefore probably like Pete. I wasn't especially overjoyed at the prospect of her sleeping with the bloke, particularly while he was trying to tax me, but then it wasn't my choice. I would have to swallow my feelings and focus upon the more immediate problem of dodging my fine. Still, no harm in trying.

'He wants you to shake your head violently, and then sprint off into the distance.'

'Shall I ask him myself then?'

'He wants to speak to you,' I admitted.

Needing no further encouragement, she skipped girlishly over to him, eyelashes batting frantically. They stood talking together. I couldn't hear what they were saying but their body language told me enough. They had obviously forgotten that I was there.

'I'll just go then, eh?' I offered.

'Yes, please,' said Pete, looking over briefly.

I left them to it. I met Ira later by the pool and she had arranged to go out with Pete that night. I voiced my disapproval at her siding with the enemy. She countered that going out with Pete would give her an opportunity to influence him while his guard was down. I chose not to answer this and mentioned, in a juvenile manner, that I was going out with an attractive German girl that night. I was trying to make out that it didn't affect me whether she went out with Pete or not. I left her and went back to my own apartment feeling most unhappy about the situation. On the way I stopped off at company accommodation and organised myself a German date for the evening, in order to back up my story to Ira.

In Strikers that night I smoked a few spliffs and tried to concentrate on the girl in front of me. Her name was Nadia and she was a lovely person. Despite her charms, my mind kept drifting off into dark thoughts about Ira and Pete.

I thought that it was my drugged-up imagination playing tricks on me, when through the smoke I saw the two of them heading across the dance floor towards me.

'Ah, there you are Barry. We need a lift to my house,' Pete told me imperiously.

I nearly choked on my beer. This really was adding insult to injury.

'What?' I managed.

'Ira and me. We need driving to my apartment,' Pete clarified. I realised then that Pete had no idea that I had any kind of involvement with Ira. Not that it would have made any difference. Ira looked uncomfortable but said nothing. Feeling thoroughly resentful, I told Nadia what was happening and we all drove back to Pete's place. He informed me that my first instalment was due in one week as Ira snuggled up against him in the back seat.

I took Nadia home and went through the motions of making love, mainly so that she'd still be there for Ira to see when she came round for coffee in the morning.

Ira did indeed come round before Nadia left and neither of us mentioned our nocturnal activities. I told her that I was going to fly to England and wait for things to settle down before coming back to Tenerife. Ira said she wanted to go to Sweden and do the same.

I had one thing to take care of before I left. Oasis owed me fifteen hundred pounds in wages and spifs. I had to blag Wubbo into paying me early so that I could take my money with me.

I caught up with him in his office and told him that I was worried about not being able to pay Pete's fine. I mentioned how strange it was that a few clumpers could have such a hold over a multi-million dollar company like Oasis. Wubbo bit, and boasted that Pete was nothing to worry about. Oasis would, said Wubbo, deal with the big fellas, 'one way or another'. When he was in full flow, he mentioned that five thousand pounds was nothing to a company like this one and that he could get hold of it in two minutes if need be. I immediately asked for the money, to pay Pete off, but he said it would be counter-productive to start giving in to those kind of financial demands. I conceded that he had a point. There is no such thing as a one-off protection payment. Even so, he couldn't refuse when I asked for my wages early – not after banging on about what a financial giant Oasis was. I got the cash in an envelope and drove with Ira to the flight shop. We both booked tickets to England because Ira was unable to find a direct flight to Sweden.

Ira spent one night at my Dad's house before catching a connecting flight to her home country. I spent two weeks keeping my head down while I waited for things to blow over back on Fraggle Rock. During my vacation I tried to think of a way I could avoid paying Pete the money. Unable to come up with a reliable action plan I opted to head back over and play things by ear.

When I arrived back on the island I went to stay with Ira – who had also recently returned – in her apartment. I kept my head down by not going out to the usual bars or working any of my routine haunts. I was banking on the theory that once Pete had extorted all the money he was after from Oasis, he would move on.

My theory, to put it bluntly, was bollocks. Pete had come to some kind of arrangement with Oasis and was still there. Enquiries told me that he was going to be dividing his time between England and Tenerife for the foreseeable future. He was planning on maintaining and developing his business interests both in Spain and the UK. Protection and extortion were his main areas of growth, although he was also currently branching out into kidnapping directors of timeshare resorts and holding said companies to ransom.

Naturally I was still both unable and unwilling to pay him the five thousand pounds he wanted. For one thing, as Wubbo had pointed out, once you start paying off guys like that they see you as an easy target, to be milked as and when required.

My 'hiding' plan left a lot to be desired but it was all I could think of if I wanted to stay in Tenerife. I had to keep out of Pete's way while he was on the island. If I managed to avoid him for long enough, I felt that sooner or later he would write me off as a hopeless case. The flaws were obvious. If he let me get away with it and people found out, they might be less inclined to pay their own taxes. Therefore I could expect enthusiastic retribution if Pete caught up with me, as a shining example to the others to pay up on time.

I stayed one jump ahead of the clumpers for the next few weeks. I freelanced, sending couples into companies where the OPCs knew me and would pay me later on the same night for the business. While I was doing this I had no connections with anyone. There was no fixed time or place where Pete could catch me. I had a couple of close shaves. On at least two occasions I left a bar barely seconds before Pete came in for a drink with his boys.

I was flying by the seat of my pants and the pressure increased further when, out of the blue, Pete called a meeting of the photo team. I didn't go, of course, but my colleagues filled me in on the gist of it. Pete had gathered them all together in the Oasis marketing office, the directors of the company being too scared to stop him, and announced that the photo team had been sold to a rival company called Palm Springs. All the photo OPCs had been part of the deal and now worked for the new firm. Pete also sent a message to me via the meeting that my fine would increase if I didn't go to work for Palm Springs, as would the brutality of my beating when I was caught.

I was stumped. The devil on one side, the deep blue sea on the other. I had to go and work for them it seemed, or I would be in even more trouble. On the other hand, it would be exceedingly fool-hardy of me to be in a meeting every night where Pete could pick me off at will.

I compromised. I went and signed up for Palm Springs but I made sure that I turned up to their marketing office at odd hours whenever I went there. This way I could decrease the chances of getting caught by the clumpers.

I went to work sporadically. At least this meant that I wasn't digging my hole any deeper, given that I had complied with Pete's wishes by moving to 'The Springs'. There was an automatic ten pound fine for every meeting that I missed but I was happy to pay those. That sort of money was peanuts compared to the kind of hospital bills Pete was likely to land me with.

Time wore on and I had to face up to the fact that sooner or later Pete would catch up with me. There was a meeting, for example, every Monday morning that was compulsory for both street and photo OPCs. It was held at the Palm Springs marketing office which was in a town called Los Christianos (where I once lived with Chris) just round the coast from Playa de Las Americas. There was no getting out of the Monday meeting. The first time you missed it, you were fined one hundred pounds, twice and you were sacked. As much as I hated to be in a place known to Pete at a specific time every week, I had no choice.

Each week on my way into the room I blended into the crowd. Head down, shoulders slumped, I made my way to the back and stood by the window. I tried to will the meeting to finish quickly in order to minimise the time it afforded for Pete to apprehend me. Talking of windows, the reason why I stood by one was so that I could exit quickly through it and take off sharpish if Pete appeared in the doorway.

It was during one such meeting that my new boss, whose name

was Danny, gave out the rather unwelcome news that he had retained Pete to oversee the photo team. Pete was a very shrewd businessman as well as a hardened gangster. He managed both his villainous and legitimate enterprises with a ruthless efficiency and it was this leadership and experience that Danny was hoping to be able to call upon to optimise the performance of the photo team. Bloody good plan really, but obviously the last thing I wanted to hear. It meant that my policy of staying out of his way was going to be almost impossible to implement.

The meeting finished and, distracted by this new challenge, I ambled out of the marketing office. I hardly noticed the jostling of the other OPCs as they bottlenecked through the door on the way to their cars and scooters. I had parked my own scooter behind a bush some distance away in case Pete knew my registration number. Deep in thought, I was walking round the corner towards it when I nearly bumped into him.

Pete was standing with the three biggest, ugliest-looking clumpers I had ever seen. They were a mere couple of yards away from me in a huddle around my scooter and Pete was staring straight at me.

I knew instantly that this was it. The end of the line. There was absolutely no way out. I couldn't outrun them because there was nowhere to run to. There wasn't the slightest possibility of outfighting even one of them, let alone four. They were going to deliver on Pete's promise of violence and they were going to do it right there and then.

Suddenly I didn't feel like such a cleverdick anymore. My foolishness had caught up with me and the time of reckoning was at hand. Terrified or not, I didn't break my stride when I saw them. To do so would have revealed the extent of my fear and they would have reacted to it like sharks to blood. I walked right up to them. The set of Pete's jaw told me that no ingratiating banter would be tolerated.

'What happens now then?' I tried to sound casual.

The side of Pete's face twitched.

'We're here to find out why you don't think you need to pay your fine,' he stated menacingly.

90

I stayed silent. Out of the corner of my eye I glanced at the other clumpers as they began to surround me. I looked back at Pete. There was no trace of leniency in his expression and I suspected that the best result I could hope for was a painful beating. It was easily conceivable that I would be crippled for life, permanently disfigured, brain damaged or killed – accidentally or otherwise.

I made a determined effort to give off inoffensive vibes but, inexplicably, I found myself fighting off an attack of the giggles. Christ, not now! I thought to myself, as I fought to keep my face straight.

Talk about moments that change your life! Pete had noticed and was shaking his head incredulously. Humour began to permeate his features.

'What is it with you Barry? I don't know why but I just can't stay pissed off with you. Come over here, I want a word in private.'

The other clumpers were as dumbfounded as I was. Looking thoroughly disappointed at not being able to bash me, they grudgingly stepped aside and let me through. When we were out of earshot, Pete told me that maybe it was because I came from the same place as him in the UK, that we were connected or something. He was going to give me one last chance. He would forget about my 'tax avoidance' on the following conditions: I was to stop smoking, taking drugs and drinking alcohol; I had to eat what he told me to; and, on top of this, I had to start going to the gym with him every day.

Now at that stage in my life, I was a particularly unhealthy individual. I weighed about eight and a half stone soaking wet and I was drunk or off my nut every night. I was pasty, spotty and ill-looking. I couldn't see why he would be so concerned about my health but I took my luck where I found it and readily agreed to comply.

'Good. I know what an untrustworthy little chap you are, so you'll have to live in my house for a while where I can keep an eye on you. Move in by teatime. Here's my key.' Pete told me. And with that last instruction ringing in my ears, I jumped on my scooter and rode off.

My pals were waiting for me at the breakfast bar. They had all witnessed my encounter with Pete and his men and were eager to find out why I was still in one piece.

'Oh, I talked my way out of it,' I said airily. 'We're good mates now. In fact we're going to be sharing a gaff from now on.'

'Bollocks, what really happened? You cried like a baby, right? You cried like a baby, he got embarrassed and gave you more time to pay.'

'I don't think so,' I grinned nonchalantly. 'In fact, who wants to give me a hand moving in this afternoon?'

A couple of them helped me move my gear down to Pete's house, purely to see if I was lying or not. I gave no further explanation for the dramatic shift in my relationship with Pete. I just left everyone wondering 'how the slimy bastard got away with it this time'.

Pete's place was in a complex called Castle Harbour. It was a luxurious duplex with satellite TV, three bedrooms, video and all mod cons. I adhered strictly to the new regime of fitness. After all, it was a welcome escape from an extremely tricky situation. After the initial relief wore off, for a little while I was inwardly doubting the wisdom of giving up what seemed to be all my sources of pleasure. It was tough going, but after a few weeks I began to develop a new sense of respect for myself. My physique was gradually transforming and I started taking pride in the way I looked.

Because of my new healthy lifestyle, I found myself in a better frame of mind for work and therefore started earning more money. This, coupled with not having to pay rent or waste money on drugs or alcohol, meant that I actually got a few thousand pounds saved during this period, much to my father's delight.

I became best buddies with Pete. He had a dry sense of humour that complemented my own. I had clearly been in need of some kind of guidance and for some reason Pete had decided to take me under his wing. I know now that I was extremely lucky to have someone with Pete's strength of character take an interest in my well-being.

After a couple of months, Pete trusted me to move out of his gaff and I rented a nice little villa on the outskirts of town. Pete and I still knocked about together. He was my boss again and his current style of management incorporated distinct favouritism toward his protégé, namely me. I got the best bars to work in, time off when I wanted it, and any nice-looking new girls were shared between Pete and myself for training. Naturally this meant that we got first crack at them, much to the envy of the other lads on the photo team – especially during the Scandi season!

Ira had gone back to Stockholm by this point. I missed her a lot but I had new friends now and I tried to fill the void that she left by sleeping with other girls. I knew that this sort of behaviour wouldn't sort things out overnight – but it didn't half cheer me up in the short term!

Pete's criminal empire was growing. He was offering a protection service to all the timeshare companies on the island. I use the term 'offering' loosely. How this worked in practice was that he charged each company about one thousand pounds a week. For this they would be assigned one of Pete's clumpers. Pete would pay him four hundred pounds a week and keep the rest. All the clumper had to do was keep the OPCs in line and make sure that no-one took liberties with the company he was assigned to. So the clumper's job was to live on the island and go to the gym because the threat alone of having one of these guys after you was enough to make most people toe the line.

In addition to this, Pete also regularly flew lads over from England for 'jobs'. He ran an illegal security firm in the UK which forced nightclubs into employing door staff from among his pool of heavies. This provided him with a small army of lads who were loyal to him, without costing him a penny. He would pay their flights over when he needed extra muscle and they would stay at either his or my villa.

I often had two or three of Pete's 'soldiers' at any one time sleeping in my spare room or on my couch. They would ask me to wake them up in time for whatever villainy they had scheduled for the day and I would give them a shout on my way to work. They would borrow my kitchen knife or claw hammer to take with them if they had no tools of their own and set off to do God knows what. Pete only discussed his activities on a need-to -know basis. I mainly just went to the gym or to the beach with him and borrowed his motorbike to drive down the strip blagging girls.

Pete no longer barred me from smoking, drinking or anything else. I did relax a little on the healthy lifestyle front but body-building became integral to my existence. Even now, twelve years later, I still hit the weights three times a week.

I was working with Henk, the guy who used to be the photo team captain before Danny hired Pete to run the show. Henk had suffered a confidence crisis when he was first demoted to being an OPC again. He was used to living off his override. As a team captain, he was paid on the results of his team and didn't have to pitch any couples himself. Now he was worried in case he had lost the old magic.

Henk was one of the original superstar OPCs that had inspired me to join the photo team. He and his partner had regularly achieved forty ups per week when I first arrived at Oasis and it was obvious to me that he would get there again. I had made it my business to remotivate him and before long we were back on top. Henk and Barry were the number one team.

We hung out together after work too. Henk was about fifteen years older than me and even five years older than Pete, so he had a different idea of what sort of places to go for a night out. He was an adept gambler. As an ex-casino owner in Antwerp, he was pretty sharp at cards. I stuck to roulette whenever we sloped off to the local gambling den because any fool can be lucky at the wheel.

Henk tried to install in me a sense of taste. Being a sophisticated European type himself, he felt it was his duty to educate me. He was responsible for my spending disproportionate amounts of money on clothes, including over a thousand pounds on a watch. It all seemed ridiculous to me but I had money to burn so what the hell. I ended up, for a time at least, the picture of sophistication. This only lasted for as long as I worked with Henk. Anyone who knows me now will vouch for the fact that the world of high fashion is no longer one I visit regularly.

Toronto and Brandon had both left. Brandon had managed to get himself himself mixed up with some Christians and become a missionary in South America. Toronto had finally gone back to Canada to join the air force. In the ever-changing timeshare crowd I always tried to hang on to a reasonably stable core of friends. Toronto, Brandon and Ira had been my closest pals and I missed them intensely when they left. My inner circle of mates now consisted of Pete and Henk. There were plenty of other people to hang about with, but it was only with those two that I really let my guard down and respected to any degree. The photo team in general was a friendly bunch and we all used to get on with each other. It was kind of dull though, and Henk, Pete and I wondered how we could add a little excitement to the equation.

Excitement was to turn up of its own accord in the form of a new recruit – a wickedly amusing sex goddess called Scarlet.

Scarlet was 5ft 10in. with short brown hair and exotically dusky skin. She had huge dark eyes, legs up to her neck and breasts like water melons. It wasn't just her statistics that made her so sexy – it was the glint in her eye, a hint of deep sensuality that left all the lads dumbstruck and jockeying for position. We were making idiots of ourselves clambering over each other to try to be the first one to sleep with her.

The first time she appeared at work she was with a black guy called Cheeks. Direct questioning established within thirty seconds that they weren't lovers, after which the show began. All the heavyweight lady-killers tried their stuff but despite some innovative attempts to get her attention, no-one actually made it to the promised land. She quickly formed friendships with people in the team, including me. I still know her today and count her among my best friends, although she can be a pain in the arse from time to time.

Back then it wasn't her personality I was interested in. I, like everyone else, wanted to shag her.

In circumstances like that I normally had an advantage because Pete would team her up with me for training purposes. While learning the job she would also be observing how brilliant I was at it. I could then capitalise on the rapport built up at work and use it to ease her passage into my bed. On this occasion, much to my disappointment, Pete wasn't forthcoming with the offer of tutelage. I tried to manipulate the situation but Scarlet wisely insisted on continuing with Cheeks, whom she knew and trusted.

After a week or so, she wasn't doing particularly well at the job and Pete convinced her to try working with a more experienced OPC. I felt that I was the man for the job and put my case to Pete while we were in the gym working out. Normally he would have agreed without hesitation but on this occasion he was unusually quiet and noncommittal. Nevertheless, I felt that I had made my point and that night in the photo meeting I sat expectantly waiting to be teamed up with Scarlet. It didn't happen. Or rather, she did get a new partner but it wasn't me. I stayed behind after the meeting to harangue Pete about his decision but all this achieved was to secure myself an angry lecture about how he and he alone ran the photo team. It was not run solely as a pimping agency for a little twerp like me!

Well and truly chastised I went to work contemplating the significance of Pete's outburst. Concluding that he was just giving me a warning not to stick my nose in where his management decisions were concerned, I concentrated my attentions on preparing the strategy for my next assault on Scarlet's honour.

I had been suggesting to Pete for some time that he ought to throw a party for the photo team. Every manager did this from time to time as a way of encouraging loyalty and bonding within the team. We would take over a restaurant or bar for the evening and the company would share the expense with the manager. Food, drink and occasionally cocaine would all be laid on and people would let their hair down – even more than usual. Pete agreed that it was a good idea and I organised the event with a popular beach-front bar.

The party was one week later and, in the meantime, I hired a motorbike. I had been thinking about doing this for some time and had only recently found a firm willing to do me a good deal for long-term hire. I knew that Scarlet liked bikes and mine was a beauty. A

450cc monster called a Dominator. It made a really loud thumping noise and when you don't have to wear a helmet (Spanish law at the time) you can look quite cool on a bike if you're dressed the part.

Never having passed any sort of motorbike test, it took me a while to get used to the power difference between it and my scooter but by the time the party rolled around I had mastered the beast. I didn't tell anyone that I had hired it because I planned to make a grand entrance at the party. I deliberately arrived late to ensure that everyone, including Scarlet, would be there.

Having purposely selected a restaurant where I could pull up directly outside, I did just that. With some deep bass throttle revving I skidded sideways to a halt outside the bar, whipped my sunglasses off and dismounted. Everyone was suitably impressed and came out to admire the machine. Including Scarlet.

'Nice bike Barry! Any chance of a ride?' she cooed.

Grr, not arf! I thought. I love it when a plan comes together!

'No problem Sca,' I replied smoothly, eyebrow twitching like Roger Moore. 'In fact, why don't I give you a lift to the Veronicas after the party. We could go for a drink together.'

'It's a deal.' She smiled and we went in to join the others.

My Machiavellian orchestrations appeared to have come to fruition and I relaxed in anticipation of the joys to come. Predictably enough, throughout the evening the lads were swarming all over Scarlet. Even Pete managed to trap her in a corner for a heart-to-heart. I kept clear so that I wouldn't seem too keen. They could all get jealous later.

Gradually the party wound down. As everyone started to leave I decided it was time to make my move as well. I couldn't wait to see the other lads' faces when I rode off into the sunset with Scarlet on the back of my bike. I had to bite my lip to stop myself from grinning ear to ear as I stood up and tried to find her. She was next to Pete.

'Pete, Hi! Scarlet and I were thinking of popping down the Veronicas for a drink, so . . .'

'Yes, we were just talking about that. Why don't you set off now and Scarlet and I will meet you down there,' said Pete, casually slipping his arm round her.

I stared at him venomously.

'No, why don't *we* meet *you* down there. You see, Scarlet wants a go on my motorbike and . . .' I trailed off, realising how childish I was sounding in front of her. Scarlet appeared to feel sorry for me.

'I've got an idea,' she offered, looking at Pete. 'Barry's been dying to show me his bike, bless him, so why don't I get a lift down there with him and then afterwards me and you can go for a quiet drink together. What do you think, Pete?'

'Hang on a minute!' I interrupted. 'You're missing the point. I was actually hoping to . . . er . . . em . . .' I blushed and looked at the ground realising what I had nearly said. Scarlet looked at me sharply.

'Hoping to *what* exactly?' she demanded.

'Hoping to . . . er . . . well . . . you know!'

'No,' she said stonily. She had adopted a confrontational posture, with her hands on her hips and her head cocked to the side. 'I *don't* know. What is it precisely that you were hoping to do?' Over her shoulder Pete was making faces at me and I went even redder.

'Oh Christ!' I spluttered. 'Look, I'll see you later.'

'Oh, so you're not even going to give me a go on your bike now?' she accused. I was completely lost.

'I'm sorry, I thought that . . .' I stopped in my tracks as they both doubled up with laughter. She had been taking the piss. Not about Pete though. As soon as we got down to the Veronicas, he turned up behind us in his car and we all went to Bobby's Bar for a drink. Pete wasn't much of a party animal so I thought it would just be a case of outlasting him stamina-wise.

Sure enough, after a few dances, he was yawning and looking restless.

'Tired, Pete?' I smiled as though concerned, whilst dancing energetically to give off an altogether different message.

'Yeah, I'm going to have to fuck off soon,' he said looking defeated, when suddenly Scarlet yawned too.

'Actually, I'm quite tired as well. You wouldn't drop me off at home would you Pete?' she asked him.

'Eh?' I floundered. 'I'm tired too, you know! Why don't I take you home on my bike Sca?' I have to admit that I sounded a bit pathetic and a sixth sense told me that I had already lost this particular contest.

'Come on, Barry, be fair, you brought me down here. Now it's Pete's turn to give me a lift,' purred Scarlet, nestling into Pete's shoulder.

'Yes, be fair, Barry,' smirked Pete as he led her to his car. Bollocks! I thought to myself as I rode home alone.

The next day Pete turned up to the gym absolutely full of himself and, despite my deliberate disinterest, proceeded to confide all the details of their sexual encounter. He seemed to really like her and was seeing her again that night.

Pretty soon they were a regular couple and over breakfast one morning Pete mentioned that she was going to stay with him for a couple of days because the contract on her apartment was up and she needed to find another place to live. Some of the girls at the table started laughing quietly among themselves. Pete saw them and began to get irritated.

'What is it? What's so funny?' he demanded. They looked at him.

'Nothing, it's just . . .'

'Just what?'

'Well, it's as though you actually believed that she's only moving in for a couple of days. You think she's going to find herself a flat and move out again, don't you?'

'Yes. That's what she said. She needs a place to crash for a bit, that's all.'

'Whatever you say, Pete,' said the girls, smiling to themselves.

Six months later they were still living together and we were all best friends. A very tight-knit crew, we worked and played together. I was teamed up with Scarlet now that it was established that she was Pete's girlfriend. He knew that I wouldn't dare to make a move on her and he also made it quite clear that I was to inform him if she so much as looked at another man. This meant that I didn't hang around with Henk so much as I used to, especially in view of the fact that he wasn't interested in going to the gym with us. It was a shame because I did enjoy Henk's company.

Pete probably thought that he was doing us a favour when he allowed me to accompany Henk on a recruiting mission to find new OPCs in Antwerp.

# 7

# ANTWERP

OPCing, although financially rewarding, is demanding, high-pressure work. Over ninety per cent of the fresh young hopefuls who fly to Spain and the Canaries seeking their fortunes, return, utterly defeated, to their home countries within three months.

This high turnover of staff means that a constant supply of new people is needed to maintain the level of workforce. At the time, the method favoured by most timeshare companies for encouraging this supply, was to do seminars in the country from which they wanted to recruit. Two of the better OPCs within any given company deemed capable enough were sent over to the capital city in question. They would be given enough money to pay for the flights and hotel, to advertise in a national newspaper and to hire a conference hall for the seminar.

The usual plan of action was to go for two weeks. After arriving you booked the conference hall for the end of the fortnight, leaving two weeks in which to advertise. Hopefully you would then get a good turnout of people. One of the two OPCs would give a pitch from the lectern at the front, and depending on the quality of this some of the audience would stay behind to be interviewed. Both OPCs would share the interviewing. It was important to give the impression you were being selective but in reality you accepted anyone prepared to give the job a try. The more the merrier as far as the recruiters were concerned because they got paid one hundred pounds for each person that joined the company as an incentive to do a good job.

## BLAGGERS

Palm Springs was desperately in need of some new Belgian OPCs for the photo team. Belgian people generally speak four languages, which comes in very useful in a job like OPCing. Pete asked Henk if he would go and run the seminar because Antwerp was his home city, so recruiting the locals should be relatively easy for him. I asked if I could go, too, as I hadn't left the island in ages. Pete consented warily but warned that the trip wasn't a holiday and that we should ensure we were back at work within three weeks. We agreed without listening. Of course we would get the seminar done but that was going to have to be fitted in around having a bloody good time in what, for me, was uncharted partying territory.

Henk and I went to the flight shop as soon as we received the assignment, only to be told that there were no available flights direct to Brussels (the closest airport) for three weeks. Our spirits undampened, we went to the airport to go on standby and thus commenced the most unpleasant journey I have ever endured.

To start with, every flight we queued for was full. Not a problem, you might think, just go home and come back for flights more likely to have free seats. The trouble was that the man at the flight desk managed to convince us each time that there were sure to be vacancies on the next plane. Every time, his guarantee of seat availability on the next flight seemed so plausible that we took him at his word and ended up queuing for another few hours.

After a day and a half we were too tired to wait on standby for any more direct flights. Even though our mate Manuel at the flight desk reassured us that he happened to know for a fact that there were definitely two free seats on the next plane, we decided to book ourselves on a regular flight to Madrid. From this larger airport there would be several connections to Brussels.

Absolutely exhausted, and having been charged an extortionate price for the ticket, we were the last to check in and I couldn't help but notice that our suitcases, unlike everybody else's, weren't issued with flight number labels. I brought this to the attention of Manuel, who told me that it was because there were no more pre-printed labels.

'Relax, Señor, it makes no difference, all of the bags are loaded

102

at the same time anyway. It is impossible for them to get lost.' His explanation reassured me in no way whatsoever but there was absolutely nothing I could do about it so Henk and I boarded the plane, too tired to care.

The passenger list boasted a disproportionate number of screaming babies, seemingly unaccompanied by their parents, and I was unable to catch up on any sleep. Instead I had to grit my teeth and attempt to blot out the noise throughout the journey. My nerves were frayed to breaking point by the time we touched down in Madrid. Henk and I were grateful when we were finally allowed to leave the plane and enter the baggage reclaim area.

'I bet our bags are the last ones out,' said Henk glumly as we settled down by the conveyor-belt. We still had to purchase flights on to Brussels and could have done without a delay in reclaiming our luggage.

No such luck. Our stuff never materialised at all and after the other passengers had left we tried to find someone who could do something about it. Enquiries revealed that the bags had made their way to Venezuela. Apparently, this was our own fault for failing to ensure that the correct labels had been attached at the check-in desk. At this point frustration overcame me. I had to go and sit down and grit my teeth while Henk tried to explain to the Iberia rep how much we wanted our suitcases back. Eventually Henk gave his address in Antwerp and the rep promised to send the bags on to us when they were returned to Madrid. As consolation he gave us a little Iberia kit bag each containing a toothbrush, soap and a change of underwear. No comment. Anyhow, two days later we finally arrived in Brussels. Absolutely exhausted, we crashed out and slept for over twenty hours at Henk's parents' house. We had already decided to stay there instead of a hotel so that we could pocket our accommodation allowance.

We gradually recuperated over the next couple of days, helped by the fact that Henk's mum was giving us food every couple of hours. I don't know what it is about European mums but they seem to take enormous satisfaction from feeding people at every available opportunity. Every time I have been the guest of a friend on the continent the same thing has happened: if you happen to wander into the kitchen for a glass of water, you get pounced upon.

'You are hungry, eh? I cook you something, yes?' The accompanying look of desperation is enough to make you eat, hungry or not, just to keep them happy. Of course, there is a ceiling on how much food you can actually fit into your stomach, but Henk's mum seemed to regard this physical limitation as stuff and nonsense. If I really tried, she was sure I would always find room for another couple of cakes, or bowl of pasta. In the end, I became terrified of this tiny little woman in her sixties and resorted to creeping around the house in an effort to avoid being force-fed. My main disadvantage to this plan was that the kitchen was designed in such a way that she could see into every downstairs room while she was cooking. And she would hide. One particular time I waited until she had gone out before tentatively venturing downstairs. I called her name a couple of times on the pretext of saying good morning. I intended to relax and plan my day without having to fend off any lard-laden culinary attacks. As there was no reply, or indeed any sound at all from the direction of either the kitchen or Henk's parents' room, I considered the area safe. I sat down in the lounge and started working on my speech for the seminar, which Henk had already booked for two weeks away. I tried to concentrate on my writing but a niggling sense of unease prevented me from getting into the swing of it. I was sure that I could smell something cooking, but I could see into the kitchen through the serving hatch. The lights were off and there was no sign of any activity. Even so, I decided to investigate further, just to reassure myself.

Upon entering the kitchen I immediately felt the warmth coming from the cooker. Thinking that it had been left on by accident, I went to turn it off – when something caught my eye and I froze. Henk's mum was concealing herself behind the door. I could see her feet sticking out. I turned the light on and pretended to be getting a drink of water, thus giving her a chance to compose herself before I 'noticed' her.

'Oh, hello Vera, I didn't see you there. Are you OK?'

'Yes, I am OK,' she said sheepishly, looking at the ground. 'I am just cooking you some breakfast.'

'In the dark?'

'Er, yes.'

'Why?'

'It was a surprise,' she said brightly, regaining confidence. I looked at her warily. Clearly she was now aware that I didn't like being fed huge meals every half hour but was refusing to accept it. She was damn well going to feed me and if that meant preparing the food covertly in order to retain the element of surprise, then so be it. There and then I realised how determined this woman was to make me eat, and resigned myself to feeling bloated and getting fat during my time in her house. I could only hope that regular nocturnal abuse of cocaine would help to keep my body-fat levels down.

Thankfully our suitcases turned up within a couple of days, so we had some clothes to go out in. And go out we did. Henk made sure I had a taste of every aspect of Belgian nightlife. From eating squirrels (yes, squirrels!) in Henk's favourite restaurant to drinking the night away with local gangsters in underground casinos. Namely one 'Jeff Bannane' who, I am told, is quite notorious among Flemmish people. A couple of years ago he died in a traffic accident and every Belgian has their own conspiracy theory about it. I don't know about that, but I do know that he got us a lot of free drinks and Charlie while we were in his company.

Suffice to say that we went on a bender for a couple of days. When we finally made it back to Henk's parents' house we could have done with a good twelve hours' kip but instead we had to make do with an hour and a half because we had a meeting with the guy who was arranging the conference hall for the seminar.

It never ceases to amaze me that following a marathon drinking session you can go to bed feeling great, and yet the mere act of closing your eyes for a couple of hours' sleep means waking up feeling like a complete zombie. So it was that morning. As we used to say in Yorkshire, 'the beer monster had beaten me up, shat in my mouth and stolen all my money'.

I got up in time and as I was staggering around trying to co-ordinate my morning activities, Henk's father, Jan, cornered me. In his broken English he seemed to be talking about my fitness regime. I couldn't for the life of me figure out why he would be interested, and given that I was in a hurry tried to postpone the conversation until later. Jan was nearly seventy and cut a very distinguished figure with his enormous silver moustache. He was insistent about saying his piece and so, late or not, I had to listen. I was about to discover that Henk had not just one insane parent, but two.

Jan asked me to show him my biceps, which I duly did, and he seemed very impressed. He told me that I should keep up my exercises while I was staying at his house and that he had figured out a way of doing this. Despite my protests of being late he made me follow him into the garden. He proudly showed me a converted climbing frame that he told me Henk had used, when he was younger, to do pull-ups from.

'You can exercise here, ja? You try, you try!'

'Yes I try. When we come back from the town, I try.'

'Try now, just once. Show me you can do.'

'Really Jan, we are so late . . .' I began, when Henk interjected,

'Ah, come on Barry. I've been telling him how strong you are. One pull-up won't hurt, eh?' I took the line of least resistance and walked up to the overhanging bar. Feeling a bit stupid, I drew a deep breath and jumped up to grab it. Expecting to grip the metal firmly and pull myself up a couple of times, I was shocked to find my hands slipping on a slimy, sticky substance that had been applied to the bar. Off balance, I landed on my backside in a puddle and looked up, perplexed. Henk and Jan were howling with laughter. Jan couldn't even speak, so by way of explanation he was waving a pot of jam at me. Sure enough it was the same stuff that was now all over my hands and shirt. Henk's seventy-year-old father had actually spent time, while I was in the shower, setting up this childish prank. Upon further reflection I actually found it quite funny but at that time I had no idea of Jan's commitment to practical jokes. He was relentless. It was impossible to relax while

I was a guest in that house – if Vera wasn't trying to feed me then I could be sure that Jan and/or Henk were giggling away somewhere, plotting another hilarious trick.

I wasn't the only victim. Each night, regular as clockwork, Jan would get up in the early hours to reset the alarm on Henk's BMW. As a result, when Henk and I opened the doors in the morning the horn would beep embarrassingly for a few minutes while Henk tried to prise the new code from his father.

Jan was also particularly proud of his ability to fart on demand and would do so in my face in order to force me out of his favourite chair if he wanted to watch TV. The last straw was when the pair of them caught me out one dinner-time.

We were struggling through one of Vera's regular calorific broadsides when Henk whispered to me that my breath smelt bad and that it was putting him off his food. Thanking him for noticing, I asked him if he would like a slap round the head to accompany his meal. Henk assured me that he was serious and, if it wasn't too much trouble, would I mind nipping off to brush my teeth before resuming eating. Jan and Vera were nodding in agreement and so, feeling paranoid, I concluded with horror that it must be true. Ashamed, I made smartly for the bathroom where, having coated my brush with toothpaste, I began a vigorous assault on the problem. As I brushed I began to notice a strange taste in my mouth. It was soap and what was more, all the bristles were coming loose in my mouth.

'Arrgh, yuk!' I spat, as I swilled from the tap, attempting to expel the mess. 'You're all fucking mental cases!' It turned out that Jan and Henk had cut all the bristles from the brush, moulded a thin layer of soap onto the brush head and then laboriously stuck the bristles back into the brush. That was when I realised that I was being seen as an easy target and would have to seek revenge if I had any hope of surviving the Dommenschrat family's hospitality.

I gave Henk and Jan no indication that I was on their case. Being a novice at this game I didn't want to give them a chance to prepare themselves. My opportunity came the next night. We had all settled down to watch *Blackadder*, which is apparently very popular in Belgium, when Henk asked me if I would go and get us a couple of beers from the fridge. I asked Jan if he wanted one too and he grunted a 'ja'. After opening the cans I had a quick check to make sure that the others weren't paying me any attention as I reached for three clean glasses and a bottle of cooking oil. I scraped as much foam as I could from the top of the beers onto a plate before pouring the beer into the glasses. Then I tipped a one centimetre layer of oil onto the top of two of the glasses and covered all three with foam. A broad grin on my face, I returned to the living-room and distributed the beer accordingly.

'A toast to, er, Belgium!' I proposed heartily. They looked at me with sceptisism.

'It's an English thing,' I explained. 'You have to take a big swallow to bring us luck for our time here.'

'A big swallow?' Jan asked, gaining enthusiasm.

'A big swallow!' I assured him and to illustrate I held my nose, closed my eyes and chugged down half a glassful. I wiped my lips and cried 'To Belgium!' again and stared at them expectantly.

They touched glasses, roared 'To Belgium!' and cheerfully threw the liquid down their throats. I savoured the next few seconds as I watched their expressions changing from good humour to disbelief and then choking nausea. They rose as one, hands clapped to their mouths, and the race was on to find somewhere to vomit. Henk made it to the kitchen sink first, so Jan had to push past him to the front door and throw up in the street, much to the disgust of passers-by.

It took a while for us all to settle down again that evening. Jan kept chuckling and wagging his finger at me and I detected a new respect in his manner. Several times I caught Henk giving me reproachful sidelong glances but he said nothing. I settled back to enjoy my beer. I had made my point and for the rest of my stay in Antwerp Jan restricted himself to the occasional trouser-cough when he needed someone to give up his chair.

The seminar went well and we sent fifteen new recruits over to join Pete's photo team. We should have flown back with them but we still had plenty of money left, so we thought we might stay until we spent it. We knew that we had a good bonus waiting for us when we got back, so we had no qualms about blowing our recruiting allowances.

For anyone who has not been to Antwerp, I strongly recommend it. The nightlife is as weird and diverse as anywhere I've ever seen and Henk's pal, Jeff Bannane, got us in everywhere without paying or queuing, which is a real bonus in any capital city. After the early bars we usually headed to Jimmy's. This was an upmarket club, very expensive and full of Belgian movers and shakers. We would stay there until two or three before sloping off to the Café d'Anverse. This club really was a shock to my English sensibilities. A huge converted factory, it seemed, anything went: there were people in varying states of undress; some overtly consuming hard drugs; even homosexual kids who couldn't have been over sixteen were snogging in the corners. One night I even found myself dancing on the stage with the enormous figure of Grace Jones.

In the daytime, Henk insisted on waking me up and dragging me off to see his country's cultural heritage. Museums, the house where Reubens lived, and even the 'Bravo' statue of the legend that gave Antwerp its name. All well and groovy, but probably stuff that is better appreciated without a thumping headache and the constant desire to vomit thrown in.

Nevertheless, appreciate it, I did, and we spent just over two months in Antwerp. Then Henk started hinting that he would like to go to England before we ran out of money. I had to confess that the idea of seeing my friends and family again did appeal, so I agreed that we should book ourselves on the ferry to Hull.

Going by boat was Henk's idea. I wanted to go by plane but Henk insisted for two reasons: it was a lot cheaper, and he insisted that he would be able to win our ticket money back in the ship's casino. I mentioned earlier that Henk used to own a casino, so I assumed that he was planning on outplaying the relatively inexperienced croupiers at cards. Not so! Only when we were safely on board and actually heading towards the casino did he confide in me that he had a system for beating the roulette wheel.

Now I have never claimed to know a great deal about gambling but it seemed patently obvious to me that such a thing was impossible. After all, wouldn't cleverer men than us have discovered this lucrative flaw years ago? I voiced my opinion to Henk but he wouldn't hear of it.

'Barry, why don't you trust me? You know that I'm experienced in these matters,' he frowned, disappointed at my lack of blind faith.

'It's not that I don't trust you, Henk, it's just that it's not mathematically . . .'

'Those mathematicians, they talk bullshit,' he interrupted impatiently. 'Look, are you coming or not?' I opted for 'not' and went to watch a film on my own. I was hoping that without an audience, Henk would feel less inclined to throw good money after bad when his theory failed to produce the goods.

During the film I was keeping an eye out for Henk, hoping that he hadn't lost too badly at the wheel. When he still hadn't joined me by the end of the feature, I feared the worst. I made for the bar area to try and find him.

The casino was on the way and to my amazement Henk was still sitting by the roulette wheel. Far from having lost his money, he was merrily placing bets and had eight hundred pounds worth of chips stacked casually by his elbow.

'Bloody hell!' I remarked ineloquently. Henk looked up.

'Ah, Barry! I told you I had this thing worked out,' he smiled, reaching for more chips.

I didn't know what to say. Common sense told me that it had to be down to a lucky streak. I knew that. And yet, as I watched Henk play, somewhere in the shadowy recesses of my mind greed wrestled briefly with, and swiftly overcame, logic. I hastily set reason to one side, bought some chips and followed Henk's play, bet for bet. I was quite prepared to ignore the math as the money began piling up. In no time I had won one hundred quid. There was already a crowd copying Henk's bets and the poor croupier was genuinely flustered. She congratulated us accordingly on every win but you could see that it rankled. In the end her boss came and took over from her. He had been watching from a distance to see if he could detect any funny business but Henk's system carried on coming up trumps, even with the croupier's manager at the helm. Henk was goading him, asking him if he wanted to close up for the night and cut his losses.

To his credit the manager kept a smile on his face as he continued paying out. He gave in at about 12.30 a.m., when I was three hundred quid up and Henk had won close to a thousand.

I was feeling thoroughly jubilant in the bar afterwards but Henk remained unfazed.

'I told you that I had a system to beat the wheel,' he said. 'I worked it out when I had my casino before.' Once again I tried to explain to Henk that such a thing wasn't possible.

'We were lucky that's all. Roulette systems, along with perpetual motion machines and the rhythm method of contraception, can only ever give the appearance of working. Don't get me wrong, I'm well-chuffed that we had a result but it could easily have gone the other way.' Henk just smiled indulgently as though tolerating the ignorance of a child. Exasperated, I looked at him.

'All right then, clever bastard, why don't you just play the wheel every night and make our fortune?'

'There is more to life than money, Barry,' he sighed. 'I come to casinos for fun. That's why I usually play poker or 21. More of a challenge. On this occasion we needed a little money so . . .' He trailed off with a European shrug. I was lost for words. I couldn't believe that he was expecting me to buy this. According to him he had access to an inexhaustible supply of cash but a sense of fair play prevented him from taking advantage. Unable to convince him otherwise, I mentally resolved to make a point of visiting more casinos with him so that I could be there when his system failed. Only then would I be able to say 'I told you so'.

To this day, in over fifty infuriating joint visits to the roulette wheel, his system has never failed to win us money.

During the remainder of the journey we got into a brawl with two off-duty policemen. Just a drunken punch-up really, but afterwards they were so worried in case we lodged a complaint that they bought us drinks all the way to Hull.

Of our time in England there's not much to tell. We stayed for just under two months and spent all the money we had, having a good time. The most amusing part for me was watching Henk's European suavity totally fail in getting any down-to-earth northern lasses into bed.

Soon, we knew, we would have to go back to The Rock. We were only supposed to have been away for two weeks and we knew that Pete would throw a wobbly when we finally showed up back at Palm Springs.

# 8

# TENERIFE IV

We managed to get a couple of cheap flights back over to Tenerife. My dad knew a local travel agent who always came through with one-way tickets to Tenerife for around thirty pounds provided I was prepared to leave at half an hour's notice. As usual, he got us a good deal for a last-minute departure. Dad dropped us off at the airport and we set forth once more unto the breach.

After catching up on some well-overdue sleep, unpacking and sorting out a car, we went to find Pete. Enquiries revealed that he was in the marketing office so, with some trepidation, we went to face the music.

Pete was surprisingly calm when he saw us. Sitting behind his desk he greeted us in an offhand fashion without looking up from his body-building magazine.

'Alright lads? How was your trip?' he asked airily, as though unconcerned about our extended absence. My guard went up immediately.

'It was awful, Pete. We've been trying to get flights back over for ages but they were all full.'

'Every flight was full?' asked Pete light-heartedly, clarifying the point.

'Yes, we were phoning the travel agents every day,' I confirmed, wanting to get off the subject.

'Every flight was full . . . for four months?' continued Pete in the same vein of unnatural-sounding good humour. I sensed an impending violent outburst and concluded that it was time to shut up. I willed Henk to do the same but, despite my telepathic urges to remain silent, he ploughed on.

'Ja, you wouldn't believe how difficult it was to get our tickets, Pete. I thought that it would be easy when we got to England but . . .'

'Oh, so you've been to England as well?' observed Pete brightly.

'Christ, Henk, shut up will you!' I hissed out of the corner of my mouth. We were only supposed to have been to Belgium after all. Henk reddened and looked at the floor. We glanced at each other and then at Pete, bracing ourselves for the bollocking that seemed to be on the cards.

Pete shrugged indecipherably and chuckled.

'Don't worry lads, you're not in any trouble. As long as you had a good time that's what's important. At least you're here now. No doubt you're eager to get back to work, eh?'

'You bet,' I agreed, relieved at apparently being off the hook. I nudged Henk and indicated towards the door. Now seemed as good a time as any to scarper while the going was good. Henk took the hint.

'Thanks for being so understanding, Pete,' he said, as we began edging towards the exit. 'I can imagine that a lesser manager might have been upset with us for being away for so long without permission. Still, we'd better be off. Things to do, people to s . . .'

'. . . Yes, eager to get back to work . . .' Pete continued as though thinking to himself. There was an edge to his voice which cut straight through our blatherings and stopped us in our tracks. Anxiously we turned to hear him out. Pete had been studying his nails as he spoke but now he raised his head to look at us directly.

'. . . actually boys, I need a couple of good OPCs to pioneer a new marketing strategy that I came up with while you were away. I think that you two are just the men for the job. Whaddya say? Are you up for a challenge?' His expression demanded an answer. I realised that we were being railroaded into something but in view of our recent four month skive it seemed prudent to take the line of least resistance. Anyway, new marketing strategy? How bad could that be?

'We're your boys, Pete,' we said bravely. 'What will we be doing?'

'Oh, I'll fill you in on the details later,' he said mysteriously. 'Go and finish unpacking your stuff now, and report to me in the marketing office tomorrow morning, we'll discuss it then.' He motioned us to leave. When the door was safely shut we both heaved sighs of relief. We seemed to have gotten away scot-free. Slapping each other on the back, we were turning to walk off when Pete shouted one last muffled instruction after us.

'Just before you shoot off lads, nip into my secretary's office and collect your chicken suits.'

Chicken suits? I thought. Why on earth would we need chicken suits? Then it hit me. Pete was toying with us. He had no intention of letting us off so easily. He had some elaborate punishment up his sleeve and whatever it was, it involved Henk and I dressing up as chickens.

Deflated, we signed for the suits from Pete's smiling secretary. She could not or would not tell us what was going on and so, the next morning, we had no choice but to report to Pete at the appointed time, wearing the designated apparel. It turned out that we were to be the first Palm Springs 'Chicken Boys'. We were to stand on the main strip from nine to five every day giving out scratch cards to holidaymakers. We were surrounded by piss-taking OPCs who all worked in the area. Bunking off wasn't an option because Pete always breakfasted in a café overlooking the strip. It was highly embarrassing and made even more so by the fact that we had to say 'Cluck! Cluck! How's your luck?' every time we gave out a card.

For one whole month, our punishment dragged on, and I have to say that we learned our lesson. Henk suffered even more than me with the pain of having to leave his expensive Italian suits in the wardrobe in favour of the big feathery costume. Still, I could remember a time when punishment from Pete would have taken a more physical form. He couldn't allow people to take the piss, friends or not, and we realised that he was actually doing us a favour by penalising us in this manner. At the end of the month we were reinstated to the photo team, but before that my path was to cross once more with the two reporters, Jan and Andy, who had stitched me up on the Costa.

One afternoon while I was asking Henk for a new pack of scratch cards I felt someone tugging at my wing. I turned to see who it was and found myself face-to-face with the pair of them. At first I didn't recognise them. Then it clicked. These were the two people who had inadvertently placed me in extreme personal danger a couple of years ago. In a fury I whipped my costume head off, then quickly replaced it when I noticed Pete scowling at me over the top of his newspaper.

'You pair of bastards!' I spluttered. 'I had to leave the Costa because of that story!'

'Relax, you got five hundred quid out of it didn't you?' Jan pointed out with a smile.

'Yes but . . .'

'. . . And I seem to remember that it got cashed immediately too,' she added, not backing down an inch. I tried to marshal my thoughts. I was, after all, very pissed off with these two and had rehearsed this moment many times since the day I first saw the story in the paper. I took a deep breath and renewed my attack.

'You're supposed to be journalists. Call that reporting? You just wrote a load of old tosh and credited it to me. Thanks a bunch.'

'Barry, wake up for God's sake. You knew what paper we worked for, what did you think we were going to write?' laughed Andy disarmingly. 'How are you doing anyway?'

I stared down my beak at him. After swiftly weighing up the pros and cons of bearing a grudge I realised that it wouldn't get me anywhere. I changed the subject.

'How did you know where to find me?' I asked Jan.

'Oh, we asked around. The other OPCs told us where you were. You weren't very difficult to find you know. Why *are* you wearing chicken suits anyway?' I reddened beneath my headpiece.

'New marketing strategy,' I mumbled, looking at my feet. 'So, what are you two doing over here?'

'This and that,' Andy cut in quickly. 'Fancy going for a drink tonight?'

I wasn't sure but Henk accepted for both of us. When they left I turned to him.

'I don't know if this is a good move, Henk,' I told him. 'They're dangerous people to get involved with.' I filled him in on the story of my last meeting with them, but far from putting him off, he became more curious. Henk, despite his advancing years, was still very successful with the ladies and he had his sights set on Jan. At lunchtime I told Pete what was going on and he took it more seriously. He suspected, as I did, that Jan and Andy weren't just here for a holiday. No indeed. Two scandalmongers like that, they were here to nobble someone. Pete wanted to know who and if it affected him in any way. I was to find out and inform him immediately.

With this agenda in mind I met Henk and the reporters that evening in Rosie's Cantina.

Rosie's was a Mexican-style bar attached to the Beverly Hills Club timeshare. It was one of the places where the photo team used to meet up for a drink after work. Over a few jugs of strawberry marghuerita we would discuss the successes and failures of the night's work. Henk and I had yet to be reassigned to the photo team but we often went there to have a drink with our pals.

Pete had pre-warned the team not to talk too much in front of the reporters when they showed up. He also instructed everyone to treat him like a tourist when he came in later with Scarlet.

When Jan and Andy arrived at Rosie's we were ready for them. I simply introduced them as friends of mine. This was also Pete's strategy. Hopefully they would believe that nobody knew who they were and that the OPCs would therefore talk freely in front of them.

Jan and Andy were the life and soul of the party. They made out that they were a married couple on holiday. They said that they were well-off, owning their own business, and insisted on buying drinks for everyone. While they were chatting I nudged Henk. I had seen Jan surreptitiously reach into her bag. I stretched past her for a cigarette and casually noted that her dictaphone was running. Henk and I exchanged glances and prepared ourselves for the subtle interrogation that we knew was about to start. Jan didn't disappoint us.

'Seeing as you guys all live here, maybe you can help us,' she smiled at the photo team in general. 'Andy and I are looking to buy property over here. What do you think about timeshare? Is it a good deal or not?' Gotcha, I thought. It was a good job I knew who they were and had prepared my pals for them or we might all have found ourselves talking too much. As it was, these OPCs were more than capable of dealing with the situation. They talked endlessly about how the industry was regulated now and how there were no more gangsters left in the business. They told Jan that they were all paying taxes these days and had to adhere to a strict behavioural code. OPCs nowadays had to pass through a rigorous interview procedure and could be deported for any kind of professional misconduct. They painted an entirely sanitised picture of OPCs constantly helping and being polite to tourists in order to promote wholesome timeshare companies who gave nearly all their profits to charity anyway.

By the end of it all Jan and Andy were scowling. They had been spending their expense money buying us drinks in the hope of getting enough dirt on timeshare to write up some kind of story. When they realised that they were getting nowhere, they confessed their real identities. Everyone pretended to be surprised but stuck to their story. As the saying goes, you can't blag a blagger, and it would take more than a change of tack to trick these guys into dropping themselves in it.

'Oh dear!' said Kate. 'I bet you were hoping for some juicy gossip about timeshare, weren't you? Sorry, love, but the business has changed. It's all above board these days.' She smiled, not unsympathetically, and offered them more marghuerita.

Jan and Andy were suspicious that I had prepped everyone and said so.

'Do you take us for idiots?' asked Andy. 'We get people ringing the newsdesk all the time with horror stories about how they've been ripped off by the timeshare companies. There's a story here and we're going to find it.'

'Some people just like to talk,' I told them. 'Most of the couples in here own timeshare in the Beverly Hills Club. Why don't you ask them if they are happy?'

At that point Pete and Scarlet walked in, wearing Beverly Hills Club t-shirts and looking for all the world like tourists.

'We're happy,' chipped in Pete. 'Best move we ever made, buying timeshare.' Then, pretending not to know us, he introduced himself and Scarlet as having owned a timeshare at the Beverly Hills Club for the last five years. They pulled up chairs to our table in the manner of two people about to bore the pants off a crowd of strangers. He and Scarlet played the part perfectly, droning good-naturedly on about how those wonderful people at the Hills (as he liked to call it) had changed their lives forever. Soon the hacks were politely trying to escape. Pete managed to detain them for a further half-hour by purchasing another jug of marghuerita and insisting that they share it with him and Scarlet. Finally he let them go and the relief was plainly visible on Jan's face. She and Andy stood up, said that it had been nice talking to us and that they were off to bed. Henk rose as well and feigned a yawn.

'Yes, it's getting late,' he agreed. 'I think I'll pop off too.' He left with them and just as they reached the door Jan slipped her hand into his. I was amazed. I hadn't noticed Henk making a move on her but he obviously had, the sly devil. Pete clocked the hand action too, and told me to catch up with Henk and give him a quick reminder to be careful about what he said in front of Jan. I sprinted after them but they had just driven off. I jumped on my motorbike, intending to follow them, but just then a girl who was walking past commented on my bike, saying how nice it was and asking me if I would take her for a ride. No contest. One thing led to another and I ended up spending the night with her.

The next morning at breakfast Pete asked me where I had got to. I told him that something had come up but I was sure that Henk could be trusted not to talk to Jan about anything he shouldn't. Henk turned up shortly afterwards, looking most pleased with himself. Pete eyed him distastefully.

'So. Henk. Rode the reporter then did you?'

'Better than that guys,' he grinned. 'I found out what they're up to.' Jan and Andy were in Tenerife doing a story about how the timeshare industry was controlled by gangsters. Apparently a disgruntled ex-OPC had contacted her and told her all about the way things were run over here, so she had decided to follow it up. She and Andy had convinced the turncoat to go back to Tenerife with them so that he could point the finger at the big boys. They had also persuaded him to take his life in his hands by wearing a wire and trying to engage some of the nastier timeshare barons in conversation about their activities. They must have offered him a lot of money – that was a dangerous game to play. If any of them even suspected his motives he would have ended up in hospital or, worse, in a body-bag. Jan and Andy were going to be stood nearby pretending to be a couple taking photos of each other. By angling the camera slightly and using the zoom, Andy could appear to be snapping Jan while actually pointing his lens directly at the targeted villains.

It was a direct assault on the industry that supported us all and as we listened to Henk's report, resentment started building up towards the traitor who was prepared to sell us all down the river. It hit me particularly hard, remembering my feeling over the whole Costa story. Jan had taken advantage of my naïvety to get me talking. This rat had contacted her with the sole intention of making money from ruining other people's credibility.

In a fit of post-coital frankness, Jan had told Henk the name of the man who was helping the journalists. An angry mob was beginning to form in the breakfast bar as word spread regarding Henk's discovery. More and more OPCs arrived with the intention of forming a posse to try and find the offender and then give him a bloody good shoeing. We were just about to set off when Pete put a block on it all. He told us that the spy wasn't to be harmed.

In fact no-one was to have any contact with him whatsoever. Violence, he said, wasn't the answer. As much as he shared our sentiments, Pete felt that we would only be playing into the reporters' hands by beating up their accomplice. He finished by giving us a stern warning that anyone who took things into their own hands would be dealt with severely. Then he sent us all, quietly grumbling, off to work.

When I caught up with him later I asked him what was going on.

'What's with all this stuff about violence not being the answer?' I asked him during our workout. 'After all, it's your answer to everything else.' Pete looked at me sharply to determine whether or not I was taking the piss. I kept a straight face and Pete opted to take my remark at face value.

'It depends on what you think I'm trying to achieve, Barry,' he said. 'It's true that letting you lot loose this morning might have stopped those reporters from getting enough information for their story. But now I've stopped all the OPCs who work for the companies under my protection from talking to them or their stoolie anyway. The story is not the issue. There's nothing wrong with good journalism as long as it's pointed in the right direction. They're after the bad boys in the industry. Well, I've covered my tracks. If my rivals in the security business don't want to have their mugs in the Sunday tabloids, they'll have to do the same.' I looked at him, suddenly understanding. Jan and Andy didn't care which gangsters they exposed as long as they got their story. Pete's organisation were on to them. It would be a lot easier, not to mention far less dangerous, for them to try and get people from another mob talking into the dictaphone. Pete would never grass but at the same time he didn't feel it was his duty to help the opposition. Anyone who ended up with his picture in the paper was going to attract the attention of the Spanish authorities and would therefore find it difficult to operate. Pete was all for less competition in the marketplace and I couldn't blame him. His business was tough enough at the best of times.

My curiosity satisfied, I spoke no more of it. We finished the workout in silence and I reflected on Pete's foresight. People used to write him off as a mindless thug, but those of us who knew him well learned to look beyond that. He was a hard man for sure – I've never met anyone more physically intimidating – but there were many different sides to his character. In no sense, for example, was he a bully. He was never violent towards people for the sake of it.

He believed in being pleasant to people who were pleasant to him. When we were on holiday in the UK together all the old ladies on his street would tell me what a 'nice lad that Peter is' without having a clue as to how he made his money. He only hurt those people foolish enough to be standing in the way of his business interests, or those who didn't show him respect on a personal level. For him the two were interlinked. If he allowed people to take liberties in a small way then his authority might come into question and he couldn't allow that. His empire was run on fear and respect. He kept things simple by dealing with all transgressions swiftly and brutally. At the same time, he would do anything to help out a mate, provided he could find a way of doing it without people thinking he was being soft.

On this occasion, as on so many others, his judgement proved correct. By the time the story came out we had forgotten all about it. Henk and I were back on the photo team and starting to make money again. I was working with Scarlet, and Henk with his new girlfriend. At Palm Springs, Sunday was the last day of the working week. The photo OPCs had a tradition of meeting up for a spot of Sunday lunch and a few beers to mull over the week's events. I arrived late this particular Sunday and when I got there everyone was crowded round an OPC called Simon. He was reading aloud from what I realised straightaway must be the newspaper article. They had done a real number on some of the island's more notorious villains. There were names, faces and horrific accounts from holidaymakers who had found themselves on the wrong side of them. At no point was Pete, or any of the companies who paid him, mentioned. I realised that Pete had sized up the situation perfectly. Only one thing still bothered me.

'What about the ex-OPC who helped them?' I asked Pete later. 'He would have stitched you up just as easily.'

'Yes but he didn't, did he?' said Pete. 'And he hasn't got away with anything. He sold out on some heavy characters. He'll be looking over his shoulder for the rest of his life.'

Pete was right in predicting that the Spanish police would be more interested in his opposition. They had to keep their heads

122

down for quite a while. When they re-emerged, things were different. It is difficult to say what the change was. Before, the two firms had always been wary of each other, but in an amicable sort of way. Now everyone was more distant, secretive even. It was as if the article had brought home to everyone how precarious their positions on the island were. Things seemed to get more and more serious as the years went by and the opposition were getting stronger all the time. Pete suspected that, as the power struggle escalated, he would be in some personal danger. He was half-right. Even Pete couldn't have predicted the chain of events that would eventually lead to his death.

I'm getting ahead of myself. Pete was going to be around for a few years yet and for now, I was still getting back on my feet financially. My stint as the Palm Springs chicken hadn't paid very well and my tastes were now quite expensive. Behind on the rent and motorbike hire, I had to put a lot of ups in over the next few weeks. Scarlet helped out by going the extra mile with me at work. Gradually I levelled out a little and settled back into my routine.

The months wore on and although I was still enjoying island life I began to question its meaning. It was as though I was getting tired of all the partying. I had these strange urges to go back to England and become part of the system. I fought the sensation as long as I could but in the end, worried that I might be growing up, I sought Pete's advice. As usual his life experience came in handy and the wisdom he imparted put my mind at rest. His solution was drastic but flawless and before he'd finished speaking my mind was made up.

'Relax,' he told me. 'You're not maturing or becoming responsible or anything like that. You just haven't worked in England for a few years, so you've forgotten how awful it is over there. It's like your schooldays. Everyone waffles on about how they're the best days of your life but when you were actually living them, they were crap. My advice to you is to go back and try living there for a bit.'

'Go back?' I asked, inviting clarification. I could already guess where he was heading with this but I wanted to hear him sound out the logic.

'Yes, really. Let me put it this way. If you do stay here you'll be demotivated for work. The idea will take root in your mind that you'd be happier living in the UK. You won't earn jack-shit on the photo team if your mind's not in it anyway, you know that. So why not give it a go back home? Who knows? You might decide to settle there. Personally I reckon you won't be able to stand the filthy weather and having to work forty hours a week for a pittance, for more than a month. I think it'll be good for you. It'll make you appreciate Tenerife more when you do come back.'

I agreed with him entirely. He had put my mind at rest and now I had a plan. I finished the week off, said my goodbyes and toddled off back to Blighty.

# 9

# LOS ANGELES

Despite the speed at which I made up my mind and then left the island, it was a big decision. After all, I was planning on changing my whole way of life. When I had fled back to England previously from the Costa things had been different – on that occasion circumstance had forced my hand. This time it was my choice. I really believed that, contrary to Pete's predictions, I was going to settle down at last.

I lived out of my suitcases for a while after I landed. Playing the returning wanderer, I went up and down the country visiting friends and family, announcing that I had come back to the fold and accepting their welcomes – a final delaying tactic really before getting down to the serious business of finding a job.

My lifelong best pal, Jase, was letting me stay with him while I searched for employment. He lived in Darlington, where Pete was from. Pete was over for a holiday at the time so Jase and I were going to the gym with him. After a training session we would all go for a drink together in town. It was during one such occasion that Pete introduced me to a club owner that he provided security for. Pete suggested to him that he might like to offer me a job as a cocktail waiter while I was finding my feet in England. The chap readily agreed and asked me to come to the club in question the following morning for a chat.

It wasn't what I was looking for long-term but I was extremely grateful for the fact that I would have some money coming in while I looked for a job with more prospects.

By day I applied for jobs and went for interviews and I worked in the bar at night. The problem was that I didn't really fancy any of the positions offered. I was beginning to get itchy feet again. Jase and I had a mate who had worked in California and when he talked about it we just wanted to drop everything and go. It sounded fantastic. All the world's top body-builders trained there. Not to mention Hollywood and all those movie stars. The more we thought about it, the more attractive a prospect it became, but we were in no position to do anything about it. Jase had a good job working for the world championship rally team and it would have been daft to give that up. For my part, I wanted to at least try and make a go of things in the UK. We agreed to make the trip sometime in the future when we each had no ties. We could never have guessed just how soon that time was going to be.

Business was slow at the club. They had too many bar staff and not enough punters. One evening before work the owner called us all into his office and told us that one of us would have to go. Looking around I knew that the others had been there a lot longer than me so out of fairness I volunteered to resign. The owner was grateful. He thanked me for not making things difficult with Pete and told me I could stay on until the end of the week. When I got back behind the bar I wondered what I was going to do – no money coming in and no job on the cards. Things were looking very black and I was having a good old self-piteous wallow when Jase suddenly burst into the club with news that changed everything. I immediately knew that something was up by his expression when he reached the bar.

'Baz, you'll never guess what's happened to me today,' he said. 'I've been laid off from work.'

'You're joking,' I replied. 'So have I.' Jase looked disbelievingly at me so I reassured him that this was indeed the case. For a second we just stood there. It was written all over Jason's face that he was thinking exactly what I was thinking. No more ties. Nothing to stop us going to California now.

We both started laughing and shouting.

'We're going to America! Yee Haa!' We leapt around the room

banging into people and knocking furniture over. I couldn't remember the last time I had been so happy. I was going somewhere new and exciting and my best pal was coming with me.

The rest of the week passed like a dream. I booked my flight straightaway. Jase had a job interview in Germany which involved him working over there for a week so that they could assess him as a potential employee. They would keep the job open for him if they were impressed because they knew that he wanted to travel for a bit beforehand. The plan was simple. I was going to go over first and find somewhere for us to live. Hopefully, I would be able to suss out a couple of jobs too. Jason was going to catch up as soon as he got back from Germany.

Simple huh? Well, I'll tell you, things looked a little more complicated when I landed at Los Angeles airport – otherwise known as LAX. All I had with me was two hundred quid. It was the middle of the night and the place looked a bit unfriendly to say the least. The airport was twenty miles from town and I didn't even know where the bus stop was, let alone which bus to catch. I had been flying for eighteen hours and needed a shower and a kip, so a place to stay was a rather urgent priority. A policeman told me where the bus station was and I decided to take the bus to Venice beach. This decision was based purely on the fact that I had heard of the place before. It was regularly featured in body-building magazines as the home of Gold's and World's gyms. The bus driver knew of a hostel on the intersection of Venice and Lincoln and I got off at the nearest stop. Ten dollars a night seemed reasonable so I checked in, showered, stashed my stuff in the locker provided and went to the pool room to begin the process of making new friends and contacts. The hostel was run by a German chap called Klaus. He was a stereotypical blond-haired, blue-eyed Aryan and all his staff were European travellers. They were easy going and friendly and I shot some pool with them and had a few drinks. By the time I went to bed I had secured myself a job as night security for the hostel. The position entailed my keeping an eye on the place between the hours of 10 p.m. and 2 a.m. It paid seventy bucks a week and came with free accommodation. The immediate pressure off, I had a damned good kip before it was time to explore my new world the next morning.

The hostel was large and comfortable. It boasted, along with the pool room, a satellite TV lounge, beer garden, self-service kitchen and laundry. It was located a few minutes' walk from the sea and about thirty miles from Hollywood.

It was only when I went outside that it really began to sink in: I was in America. The streets were wide, just like the movies, and the cars all seemed to be the size of buses. I recognised the names of shops from TV and magazines. It all seemed so familiar and yet strange and exciting. Feeling happier and more optimistic than I had done in a long time, I made my way down to Venice beach itself.

The beach-walk there is a surreal place: beautiful women wearing skimpy bikinis fly past on skateboards pulled by Pitbull terriers; performers juggle anything from balls to buzzing chainsaws; people on BMXs, rollerblades and even windsurfing boards with wheels gather to show off their skills to the admiring crowds.

I wandered round in a daze. I had heard that it was an amazing place but nothing had prepared me for the fluid spontaneity of it all. And everyone was so good-looking. Perfect bodies everywhere with golden Californian tans. Yes, I thought, I could get to like it here.

I needed to join a gym and ended up choosing Muscle Beach. This is a famous open-air gym right on the beach itself. Arnold Schwartzenegger and all the famous body-builders of the '70s used to train there. It was now a Californian landmark and was subsidised by the city council. The cost was only fifty dollars per year for membership and, given that it was an open-air gym, it was ideal for getting a tan while you worked out. There was also the added advantage of admiring girls watching you as you hefted the weights.

It was going to be another couple of weeks before Jase arrived so I had plenty of time to get into the swing of things. Seventy dollars a week was obviously a lot less than I was used to living on but it was more than enough. The cost of living was about a quarter as expensive as it was in the UK. I was only spending fifteen dollars a week on food and that was considered a lot. Still, it's in my nature to hustle when I can and Klaus' crew showed me the ropes when it came to working the scams. The first thing I learned was that you didn't pay for telephone calls. Most nights you could rely on a bloke called Anton to come round the hostel selling 'magic numbers' to people he knew and trusted. You paid him ten dollars and he would give you a code to tap into the phone before you dialled, enabling you to call anywhere in the world for as long as you liked, free of charge. The magic numbers had a limited lifespan. You usually got a couple of days out of them before they stopped working and then you would have to buy another. Anton was a drug addict and even though we suspected that his sources for these numbers may have been illegal, in the absence of any proof we had to assume otherwise. Innocent until proven guilty, right? Anyway, the maths worked like this: staff members would buy the original number for ten dollars; after making all the calls that they wanted to on that particular night, they would then hustle all the Aussie travellers in the hostel and would charge them ten bucks for each call. That's still a very good deal for a call of unlimited duration to Australia from the USA. There were four payphones in the hostel and you could generate a queue of five or six people at each one for a good day and a half. From an original investment of ten dollars, your return would be about one thousand. I am not saying that I ever took part in this scam mind you – I might want to go back to America one day and I certainly don't want the FBI on my case.

Other ways of making money included hiring out bicycles. We bought bikes across the road at the second-hand shop for between ten and twenty dollars, and then rented them out to the travellers staying at the hostel for an easy ten bucks a day. Most of the business opportunities at the hostel were sewn up by the assistant manager. His name was John but we called him 'Bigfish', short for 'big fish in a small pond' because he liked to act important and revelled in the power of his position. He sold trips round the stars' homes for thirty dollars a shot. This involved paying him to drive you round Bel Air and Beverly Hills following the route of a photocopied 'star map' that you could buy at any corner store for a few cents. He also made a nice little packet from the weekly barbeque that he organised. They were always sold out. For five bucks you not only got all the food you could eat, but all the beer you could drink too. It even attracted people from all the other hostels in the area and thus helped me out, by feeding my now insatiable appetite for young female travellers.

Suffice to say that I was well into the swing of things by the time Jase arrived. I had been using magic numbers to keep in touch with him and I knew that he was going to love the place as much as I did.

I couldn't meet Jason at the airport because I was working but one of the lads picked him up in Bigfish's car. He was as impressed with the place as I was and quickly made friends with Klaus and the boys. In no time he was on the payroll and we could concentrate on enjoying ourselves.

The next few months were among the most enjoyable of my life. Most days we would get up around ten o'clock, pull on a pair of shorts, add some shades and cycle down to Muscle Beach. We would work out first thing in the morning and then head off to the beach or wander around taking in the sights for a few hours. Then we would work out again, stop off for a 'Venice Smoothie' at one of the beach-front milkshake bars and hang out for a bit, before cycling back to the hostel to plan the evening's activities.

Sometimes, for a change, we would cycle over to Hollywood and mooch around the strip. We used up a lot of camera film at the Chinese Theatre, particularly when we were lucky enough to see a car chase being filmed on the streets nearby. The one thing that surprised me about Hollywood was how poor the area seemed. You only had to walk for a couple of streets off the main strip and it degenerated into a quagmire of Hispanic ghettos. There also seemed to be a high percentage of crazy people and winos on the strip itself. It didn't bother Jase and I too much when we were there together but on one occasion I went with a girlfriend it was a different story.

Martja was a beautiful Dutch girl who had been travelling with her boyfriend. Unfortunately, he'd been required to go back to Holland early to sort out some problems with his business but had insisted that Martja stay and enjoy herself for the last few weeks of the trip. Anyone, boy or girl, who leaves their partner alone in another country is asking for trouble, in my opinion. I swooped in on her in much the same way as a hawk swoops in on a rabbit exposed in an open field and, as far as I was concerned, was simply enjoying the fruits of her boyfriend's stupidity.

We did the bike ride to Hollywood together because she had never been before. She was most impressed with it all until a dirty great vagrant started getting on her case.

We were walking hand in hand down the strip, reading the stars' names on the pavement, when I noticed her expression had suddenly changed. Looking round I realised that what I had thought was an innocent passer-by was in fact a rather off-putting wino. He was walking alongside her, muttering and drooling.

'Can I feel your breasts?' he was asking. 'Go on, it won't hurt, and then I want to reach into your shorts and . . .'

'Now look here,' I exclaimed, turning on him. 'Perhaps you didn't realise but that's my girlfriend and I'd really rather you fucked off and left her alone.' I eyeballed him until he backed down.

'Sorry man, I don't know what came over me,' he said, suddenly sounding completely reasonable. 'I didn't realise you two were together. I'll go and get my own girl, huh?' Martja huddled close to me as we watched him amble off. Thinking that I had dealt successfully with the problem we set off on our way, when there he was again. He had caught up with us and was walking about a foot behind Martja, talking into her ear.

'Yeah, if you like we could go to this place that I know near here and you could suck my . . .' Martja was cringing and looked to me for help. I could see that the man was ill but I was more worried about Martja's feelings at that moment.

'You again. Look pal, I don't care if you're sick, drunk or whatever. If you don't fuck off and leave my woman alone I'm going to knock you spark out. Now scarper!' The man seemed to recognise us and appeared thoroughly contrite.

'Jeez, I'm so sorry. I guess I'm bothering you, huh? Don't you worry little lady, I'll be on my way now. You two lovebirds enjoy Hollywood on this fine day.' He shuffled off in the opposite direction and we watched him disappear into the crowd. For the next five minutes or so Martja kept glancing over her shoulder as we walked, but gradually she relaxed. We went to look at the film stars' handprints at the Chinese Theatre. I wanted to get a photo of the section where Marilyn Monroe had inscribed, 'Gentlemen prefer blondes' next to her tiny indentations. I had always been a fan and this would take pride of place in my memorabilia collection. We got the picture and Martja was laughing and joking again. She was pretending to be jealous of the long-dead sex symbol and was playing for affection, when, unbelievably, our friend turned up again. This time he grabbed Martja's arm to get her attention and launched into another silver-tongued barrage.

'Right, that's it!' I told him. It was a beautiful left hook. He was unconscious from the moment of connection and landed in a stinking, crumpled heap on the sidewalk.

Sometimes you can't do right for doing wrong. The crowd around us thought it was all in very bad taste.

'Hey, buddy, he's just a tramp. He doesn't mean any harm,' said one bearded Texan with a camera hanging round his neck.

'He was hassling my girlfriend. Anyway, mind your own business, you silly looking cunt,' I retorted, deciding that I had no reason to be on the defensive.

'Oh, he must be one of those English "hooligans" we keep reading about,' announced a middle-aged man to his wife as they turned on their heels in disgust. The crowd of onlookers began to break up but now we had a new problem to deal with. Out of nowhere, a posse of hobos was gathering together. Some of them were attending to the guy on the ground but most of them were pressing in our direction. A few of them were young and relatively fit-looking and all of them looked like they wanted a piece of me.

'Let's get out of here,' said Martja. We backed away, then turned and ran to where our bikes were chained. We had left them down an alley halfway along the strip. I was in a hurry to undo the padlocks and scarper because the alley came to a dead-end. I tried to stay calm as I wrestled with the keys. After what seemed like ages we were on our way, furiously peddling towards the entrance of the alley, but we weren't quick enough. Before we made it to the exit the tramps had caught up with us. Blocking our escape route they were walking menacingly towards us, and seemed to grow in number all the time. I knew that we would have to act quickly or all would be lost.

'Get behind me,' I shouted to Martja. 'I'm going to smash through the middle of them.' I raised my bike above my head, intending to use it sideways on as a sort of snowplough cum battering ram. I took a deep breath and readied myself for the charge.

Luckily I didn't have to. From the end of the alley the short bursts of a police siren diverted everyone's attention. A patrol car had pulled up and its occupants were keen to know what was going on. A voice over the loudspeaker demanded that we all remain exactly where we were. Only Martja and I complied – the hobos scattered in all directions and within seconds it was as if they had never been there at all.

The police questioned us perfunctorily but were happy to accept our story that the tramps were just trying to nick our bikes. I suppose that they had more important things to be getting on with, as did we. We laughed about the incident on the way back to the hostel but privately I resolved to be more careful in this dangerous city.

One person who never worried much about 'being careful' was a friend of Jason and I's called Crazy Eddy. A Puerto Rican immigrant living on a boat at Marina del Rey, he was a regular visitor to the hostel and his mad antics shocked even us. He was a tiny little fellow, aged about twenty-eight years old. As the manager of a local record shop you would think he was a responsible and professional citizen, but his behaviour outside of work suggested an entirely different character.

The first time we met him he was sitting outside in the hostel beer garden. Klaus introduced us and we found him pleasant and amiable. We had a few drinks with him and later on, when Jase and I were feeling peckish, he offered to cook for us. We accepted, thanking him, and he disappeared into the kitchen. Less than two minutes later he was back with a bottle of soda water and some bread. Jase and I looked questioningly at him.

'Is that what you meant when you said you'd cook for us?' I asked. 'Getting some bread and water out of the kitchen?'

'Say, you boys really underestimate American hospitality, don't you?' he said, shaking his head. 'As if I would give you bread and water. Watch and learn. We're having pigeon casserole tonight.' As he spoke Jason and I noticed ominously that there were, in fact, a few pigeons nearby in the car lot. Eddy dipped a chunk of his bread in the soda water and threw it towards them. He did it again and a couple of the birds gobbled down the wet crusts. Eddy stepped towards them sharply and they all rose into the air. Seconds after take-off the two pigeons that had eaten the bread exploded. Yes, exploded! There is no other way of putting it. Both birds dropped to earth in a puff of feathers and Eddy scooped them up triumphantly by their feet.

'Ha ha!' he screeched. 'In the pot for you!' and scurried off to the kitchen. Klaus told us that it was something to do with a pigeon's digestive system. Its innards couldn't cope with the bubbles in the soda apparently. Either way, Jason and I had no intention of eating those birds having witnessed their gruesome killing. We bolted while Eddy was still in the kitchen and stayed away from the hostel for a few hours. By the time we returned the casserole was gone and the rest of the staff was looking a bit green around the gills. Eddy had made everybody try some before telling them what it was. There had apparently been quite a queue for the toilets and not everyone had been able to wait. Enough said.

Eddy had plenty of tricks up his sleeve and would go to any lengths to provide entertainment. His way of meeting girls was to fall off his push-bike at breakneck speed in front of them, making it look as though they had caused the accident. He liked doing this on the cycle path at Venice beach where there was always a crowd.

Nine times out of ten he would at least elicit some sympathy and when he did he was like Flyn, to coin a phrase. He considered the risk of personal injury a small price to pay for the actual results, and Jase and I did nothing to dissuade him. After all, he usually targeted groups of women which meant that there were plenty to go round.

Of all his stunts, my personal favourite was the one he called 'the barnacle'. This dangerous but highly amusing spectacle was specifically designed for the Los Angeles cross-town bus. We would all get on together but Jason and I would sit away from Eddy, as if we didn't know him. Eddy would choose the seat directly behind his intended barnacle victim, usually a middle-aged single man. At some point during the journey, completely without warning, Eddy would casually reach forward and clamp his hands over his victim's ears. The dupe in question would panic and try to remove them. Eddy would say nothing and would steadfastly refuse to be pried from his terrified target. Sometimes the struggle would be extremely violent and would involve several other passengers coming to the aid of the victim but Eddy never gave up. He would only relinquish his vice-like grip when the driver actually stopped the bus and threw him off. Jase and I were there to make sure that Eddy didn't get hurt during all this. In a city where people went out of their way to avoid even passing contact with strangers it is easy to imagine how disconcerting it all must have been for the 'barnaclee'.

We packed a lot into our time in America. We drove to Las Vegas, San Francisco and even briefly crossed the Mexican border. We camped one night on the very edge of the Grand Canyon and watched the shadows creeping over the Colorado river as the sun went down. We went to Magic Mountain, Knottsberry Farm and Disneyworld. We had our pictures taken with ET and Jaws at Universal studios. The pièce de résistance though was the morning we went to Gold's Gym at eight o' clock and met Arnold Schwartzenegger.

The lads at the hostel had told us that Arnie worked out there every day, usually around that time. We suspected that it was a wind-up to get us out of bed early and send us on a wild goose chase, but we cycled down there anyway. Arnie was a big deal to us – he was the most successful body-builder in the world and, at that time, he was the most successful movie star too.

We locked our bikes up outside Gold's and, feeling a bit foolish, we went through the main doors surreptitiously glancing this way and that. We didn't have to look for long however, as just round the corner from reception there he was, right in front of us, the man himself, doing a set of bicep curls. No-one else in the place was paying him any attention. Maybe they all knew him or maybe they were just more sophisticated than us. Jase and I just stood there with our jaws hanging slackly open until he finished his set. It must have been hugely irritating for him, but he handled it well – he locked eyes with us like the Terminator he was and said, 'What can I do for you boys?' in his strong Austrian accent. We didn't have a clue what to say. We stood there gulping stupidly. Jason realised that I was as stuck for words as him and quickly muttered that we had come for a workout.

'Well, go and get changed then,' was Arnold's advice. We retreated hastily, paid the receptionist for a session on the weights and went to the locker room. We were kicking ourselves as we got changed. We had just met the most famous man on the planet and had effectively blown our chance to get so much as a photograph to prove it. Who would believe us when we got back home? Fortunately for us, as well as being a big shot movie star and one of the richest men in America, Arnold Schwartzenegger is also a nice guy. He knew that we were just a couple of fans who wanted to see him, so he followed us into the locker room for a chat. He sat down with us for about twenty minutes chatting about movies and body-building. He signed our t-shirts and posed for photos with us. By the time we left the gym we felt like we knew him really well and it was definitely one of the high points of our adventure in California.

Jase had to leave Los Angeles after a few months. He had decided that it was time for him to get on with his career and had accepted the job in Germany. I knew when he left that I was going to miss him, and I did. I began using the magic numbers more to keep in touch with Pete and Scarlet. For a while they were both talking about coming over to do some travelling with me in America. Pete dropped out, knowing that he couldn't keep a tight rein on his protection rackets from another continent. Scarlet wouldn't come without him and in the end I was thinking about leaving the place myself.

Pete picked up on my mood the next time I phoned him and once again he was there with sympathetic advice and support. 'I think it's time you came home to Tenerife,' he told me. 'You've had a great time in Los Angeles but it's not in your nature to bum around permanently. You need the challenge that you get from working in timeshare. You've had some time out and recharged your batteries, now it's time to get back to work. The photo team needs you and besides, your friends all miss you. Whaddya say?'

'What *can* I say?' I choked. 'You're absolutely right. I'm on my way.' I made arrangements to meet him in Darlington just as soon as I could book myself a flight home, and hung up. As I turned away from the phone, relief washed over me, I knew that the decision to leave was the right one and it felt good to have made up my mind. As I was closing my address book I noticed a number that Ira had given me for her parents' house in Sweden. I still had plenty of free phone time left so, on a whim, I dialled the number.

I pretty much knew that there was very little chance Ira would actually be there. I hadn't spoken to the girl in years and I knew that she didn't like staying in one place for too long. Her father answered. He hadn't spoken to her for a while either but he did have her current phone number in Stockholm, where she was working as a waitress. Ira's dad seemed to be missing her and asked me to give her his love when I got through.

I dialled the new number. I felt some trepidation as it rang at the other end. I didn't know if she would remember me or, if she did, whether she would welcome the intrusion into her new life? Suddenly the phone connected and a female voice said something in Swedish. I knew straightaway it was her.

'Ira,' I said. 'It's Barry. How are you?'

'Barry? Barry from Tenerife?' she asked, stunned. 'Jesus, how are you? I haven't heard from you in ages. How did you find me?'

'Find you? Why, were you hiding?' I asked, indignant.

'Now you know I didn't mean that,' she said patiently. 'It's just that I've been to so many different places since I left Tenerife I'm surprised you managed to track me down. How come you didn't call me before?' I explained myself, rather well I thought, and asked her what she had been up to besides waitressing. As she was talking, all my old feelings for her came flooding back. When the phone call drew to a close she asked if I'd like to visit her in Stockholm on my way back to the Canaries. I accepted immediately.

'Yeah, why not? I could stop for a week or so I guess. It'll be interesting to see how much fatter and older you're looking these days.' Ira rebuked me but said that I could stay for as long as I liked. She reckoned that she had enough connections to get me a bar job so that I wouldn't waste too much of my depleted funds while I was there. I told her that it all sounded very good to me and that as soon as I got back to the UK I would book myself on a ferry over to Sweden. The outcome of all of this was that I had made a decision that was to delay my return to the Canary Islands for another six months.

# 10

# STOCKHOLM

Getting back to Britain was more than a bit hair-raising. I bought a return ticket to Heathrow from a Mexican chap I knew in the hostel: Fransisco Hernandez was his name, and he only wanted a hundred bucks for the flight. In those days travel agents refused to change the name on a ticket after it was issued, preventing the traveller from selling an unused section of a return journey. However, there was a common enough trick that most people used to get round the problem, which worked like this: firstly the named person on the ticket would accompany you to the airport; he/she would bring their passport and check-in your luggage as if it were their own; after this you would both head in the direction of the departure lounge while it looked to any casual observer like you were just walking with them to say goodbye, on the way they would slip you their actual boarding pass and you would hand over in return the money agreed for the ticket. At no other stage of the journey was your boarding pass checked against your passport, so, as long as you were discreet about handing over the cash for the pass, you were home free. We used to do this in Spain all the time but I think at that time the Americans were experimenting with new procedures to try to close the loophole. Judging by how close I came to getting caught, I may well have been one of the last few people to leave the USA on a false ticket.

It all seemed to be going to plan. Fransisco checked my bags in and handed over the boarding pass without incident. I paid him his dough and said goodbye. Relaxed, I breezed passed the security checkpoint where they X-ray your hand luggage and continued on towards the departure lounge. I bought a couple of magazines from the bookshop and settled down while I waited for my boarding call.

When my flight number was finally announced I made my way, with all the other passengers, to our assigned boarding gate. My mind on some business I had to take care of in the UK, I shuffled along oblivious with the slow-moving queue towards the officials checking boarding passes and directing passengers to their allocated seats. This part should have been routine but when I got closer to the front of the queue my ears suddenly pricked up as I heard one of the officials give some alarming instructions to the people in front of me.

'Once again, everybody, please have your boarding pass and your passport ready for inspection when you get to the gate.'

Bollocks, I thought, bollocks, bollocks, bollocks. They were obviously checking to make sure the names matched, and mine obviously weren't going to because I was blatantly a different person to Señor Hernandez. Our names weren't remotely similar. We didn't even come from the same continent. There was no way I was going to slip through but, on the other hand, running away would be an instant confession of guilt. Having no idea what to do I carried on moving forward with the queue. My only option, such as it was, was to act as innocently as possible and plead ignorance if required.

My turn came. My heart was pounding but I managed to adopt a bored expression as I openly displayed my passport and boarding pass to the huge, uniformed black gentleman who stood between me and freedom. He examined them and looked at me. In that instant I just knew that the outcome would be a grilling by the anti-terrorist squad followed by time in a federal penitentiary.

'Thank you, sir, have a nice flight,' he intoned, motioning me on my way. I stood there stupidly for a second before the people behind me nudged me forward with their hand luggage. To this day I'll never know how I got away with that. Maybe the official just saw what he expected to – his was, after all, a repetitive job. Maybe he felt like giving me a break. Who can say? Whatever the reason, I quickly regained my wits and strolled onto the plane, almost laughing out loud with relief.

Once on board, I found my seat and nestled into it, smugly congratulating myself on how I had fooled those stupid Americans. What had I even been worried about? I was too clever for them by ha . . .

'Would passenger Fransisco Hernandez please stand up?' an official-sounding voice on the tannoy interrupted my thoughts. Terror once again coursed through me. I hadn't got away with anything, they were just waiting until I had boarded the plane before arresting me, that way they had a watertight case when it came to court. Shakily I rose, conscious of my bleached blond hair and North-European looks.

'Si?' I said nervously, still trying to bluff my way out of it. Two grim-faced stewardesses approached me through the sea of passengers.

'We're terribly sorry Mr Hernandez, but there seems to be a problem with the seating arrangements. Would you mind changing to seat 14C? It's another window seat.' Dazed, I readily agreed. Whether by a window or not, 14C had to be better than being some psychopathic criminal's bitch in the pen. Feeling thoroughly off balance now, I took up my new position and prayed for the aeroplane to hurry up and take off. Out of the corner of my eye I could see the stewardesses. They were talking surreptitiously and looking in my direction. For Christ's sake arrest me if you're going to, I was thinking, otherwise leave me alone. They did come over again and I steeled myself for what turned out to be yet another seat change. Twice more this happened, and by the time we did take off I was a jangling bag of nerves. In the air I could finally relax. Whatever happened at Heathrow they couldn't refuse me entry.

They did not. I went through customs without incident and shaking the dust of LA from my trainers, headed North to Darlington.

I stayed with Joanne, Jason's sister. The next day I had a couple of errands to run. First I booked myself on a ferry to Sweden for the following day. Then I went round to Pete's parents' house. I left a message with them that I wouldn't be meeting Pete as arranged, and I also entrusted to their keeping my Arnold Schwartzenegger signed t-shirt which I had decided to give Pete as a present from my trip.

The ferry had no casino, so I was unable to reimburse my fare, but it was reasonably priced and I was able to invest in an extensive hangover at the 24-hour bar.

The trip lasted a day and a half, including rail travel at both ends. I made the last short leg of the journey by taxi and soon I was knocking on Ira's apartment door. I heard excited noises from inside, the sound of music being turned down and then someone galloping towards the door in high heels. It opened and there she was. Even more beautiful than I remembered and, it seemed, very pleased to see me – her welcoming smile and hug knocked me for six! I was ushered inside and introduced to a couple of friends she had invited round to meet me. The plan was that we consumed a couple of bottles of wine in the house while I got changed, and then it was off for a night out in Stockholm. I was exhausted after the journey but Ira was prepared for this and had the cocaine lined up nicely for me when I emerged from the shower.

Ira's pals were a good laugh. Sometimes you just know that it's going to be a blinding night out – a good mix of people and everyone in high spirits. That was how I was feeling as we piled into the first bar. We got outrageously drunk and Ira and I relived old times in Tenerife. We ended up in a pub where one of Ira's friends, Cara, introduced me to her boyfriend Jan, who was working as a barman. He was able to get us all free drinks and soon we could barely walk. Ira got chatted up by some swarthy-looking Arab chaps and drifted off with them. By the end of the evening she had disappeared altogether. I was too hammered to notice or care, until I remembered that I couldn't find my way home on my own and, furthermore, I had no key. In a panic I dragged Cara from bar to bar looking for her but to no avail. I began to worry aloud about where I was going to kip, and Cara generously offered the sofa at her and Jan's house. Drunk and tired, we left shortly afterwards. Jan had to finish his shift so it was just me and Cara in the taxi. As you've probably gathered by now, me and scruples don't get on very well after a few drinks and by the time we reached the house I was kissing her. We maturely agreed that it would be a bad idea to take things any further and we stuck to this theory for a good twenty minutes before the inevitable happened. Afterwards we were both wracked with guilt. I quickly shifted location to the couch and tried to look as though I had innocently crashed there upon entering the apartment. When Jan did come in, I pretended to wake up and smilingly inquired how his night had gone. He took in the scene before him through slightly narrowed eyes, as though sensing that something wasn't quite right.

'Fine thanks. And you?'

'Most enjoyable,' I replied, a little too enthusiastically. I bit my lip as his gaze flickered towards his girlfriend and then back to me.

'Cara looked after you then?'

'Oh yes,' I confirmed, fighting like a lion to keep a straight face. I could see that he was suspicious but I wasn't going to give him any clues – I was on the sofa, she was in the bed, end of story. 'Good night then,' I yawned and snuggled into my blankets, cutting short the conversation. I could hear him standing there during a few more indecisive moments, then turning on his heel and getting into bed. His silence didn't last long. I don't understand Swedish, but I could easily pick up the gist of his attempt to interrogate Cara. But thankfully she was having none of it.

'For Christ's sake, Jan, don't be so suspicious!' or its Swedish equivalent.

The next morning the atmosphere in the flat was still very tense so I quickly gleaned directions back to Ira's house and left. When I eventually found my way back, Ira was on the phone to Cara. There had been a frightful row when I left. Cara had denied everything of course, but Jan had smelt my aftershave on his pillow. I always did wear too much of the stuff. Apparently, Jan had told Cara that he was going to give me a dig when he saw me next. This was obviously bluster, if he was going to do anything he would have done it already. Ira was laughing.

'Trouble just follows you around, doesn't it Barry?'

'Don't be shifting the blame onto me,' I protested. 'It was your fault. You left me on my own with her. Where did you sleep last night anyway?' Ira shuffled her feet and claimed not to remember.

'Exactly,' I smirked. 'So get off my case.'

Thus commenced two months of drinking, drug abuse and getting into trouble. Jan was friends with some of the bouncers from the clubs nearby and they had all sworn to give me a good beating if they ever caught up with me. They never did. To be fair, I let it be known that I was carrying a claw hammer around inside my jacket – just in case – and maybe they thought it wasn't worth the effort.

A few nights after the Cara incident, I landed my first job. We were in the School Bar, situated at the very centre of Stockholm. It was summer and I had opted to display my weight-trained body by wearing a vest instead of the more conventional long-sleeved shirt. No-one noticed until I removed my jacket when we sat down with our drinks. Almost immediately a huge square-headed bouncer materialised by my side. I chose to ignore him and he eventually coughed politely and spoke up.

'Excuse me, sir, could you put your jacket on please?'

'No, I couldn't!' I said, looking round at him dismissively before resuming conversation with Ira and the others. The guy had been polite enough, but I couldn't resist the opportunity to show off in front of the girls. Anyway, Square Head hadn't been prepared for this line of response and from the periphery of my vision I could see him shifting awkwardly, unsure how to proceed. After a lapse of maybe half a minute or so, he gripped my shoulder and tried a firmer tone.

'It's just that we have a dress code in the School Bar and . . .'

'Look, cloth ears, I said no didn't I? Now fuck off!' I brushed his hand off my shoulder and obnoxiously turned my back to him once more. Square Head was at a loss. Presumably he wasn't used to dealing with pricks like me. He left in the direction of the bar and had a brief but animated discussion with an important-looking older chap who was standing near the till. Then he stomped back over with his jaw set in a determined fashion and tried again to assert his authority.

'This is your last chance,' he said. 'Either you put the jacket on immediately or I'll have to throw you out.' Now, a tough guy I am not, but in those days I was an expert at making people think I was. I knew the importance of bluffing. If I'd backed down even slightly he would have seen straight through me and I would probably have ended up picking my teeth off the floor. As it was, he was holding back because he couldn't work me out. I was a lot smaller than he was, so, to his mind, there had to be a reason why I was so confident. Maybe I was a world-class boxer. Maybe I was carrying a knife? Or maybe I was just one of those nutcases who goes berserk when challenged and doesn't stop until mortal damage has been done. I jumped off my stool and faced him eye-to-eye.

'Gonna throw me out are ya? Come on then, you plum. I bet you can't!' I stood there with my fists clenched and stared him down. He was well and truly fooled and backed off helplessly. Phew, I thought. I was wondering what to do next when Ira saved the day. She knew the owner, who, as you've probably guessed, was the chap at the bar. He and Ira stepped between myself and the bouncer and calmed the situation down. The owner told one of the waiters to bring a round of drinks to our table and then asked me in a respectful manner if I would possibly put my jacket back on as a favour to him. Glad to have escaped the situation unscathed, I charmingly complied. The bar owner's name was Johan, and he stayed for a few drinks.

'Ira tells me you were in the special forces,' he confided, when he felt that he knew me well enough to enquire. This threw me a bit. The closest I have ever come to military service of any kind was having quite a short haircut a couple of summers ago. I twigged that it was Ira's attempt to rationalise the discrepancy between my size and my attitude. I mumbled something about having been in the Paras, and that I would rather not talk about it. I wanted to change the subject as quickly as possible. When you start telling lies like that they grow and grow, and sooner or later someone with some genuine knowledge on the topic will come along and your game's definitely up, and who knows what the outcome will be.

'I see, I see!' said Johan, nodding his head conspiratorially. 'Well, Barry, Ira tells me that you're looking for a job?' I agreed that I was and Johan smiled. 'I may be able to help you there,' he told me. 'I need another guy to work on the door. Normally Sven is enough but sometimes at the weekends things can get a bit rough. I can see that you're not scared of a bit of trouble. Why don't you come down and see me on Thursday evening and we can talk about money?'

I was boxed in and had no choice but to heartily accept. I needed the work after all, but I dreaded to think what was going to happen when the first fight broke out and I folded like a paper bag. Johan brought us a bottle of champagne and went back to his duties, leaving me to reflect on the wisdom of my actions.

I needn't have worried – the next turn of events decided things for me and it seemed that I wasn't destined to work in Stockholm after all. Ira's hitherto unmentioned boyfriend was soon to learn of my presence and, while he was physically unimposing, he wielded a good deal of power among the bar and club owners in that fair city. It all started the next morning when the shrill ringing of the phone dragged me gradually back to consciousness. Groggily I sat up and looked blankly at the offending object. Ira lay motionless and displayed no intentions of answering its whining call so I reached over her prostrate form and dragged the receiver to my pillow.

'Yeah, what?' I grunted. You have to remember that Ira and I weren't working at the time and I considered a phone call during daylight hours to be the height of rudeness.

There was a frosty silence from the other end and then finally, 'Who are you?' It was a male voice and not a friendly one.

'I'm Barry. Who the fuck are y . . .'

Click, brrrrrrr.

Whoever it was hung up. Evidently they didn't want to chat. Gratefully, I crawled back under the covers, but not before taking the phone off the hook.

That evening, when we were getting ready to go out, I mentioned the mysterious caller to Ira who explained that it was probably her boyfriend, Mario. He was a big-shot restaurant owner with a chain of Italian places scattered throughout the city. Ira hadn't mentioned him until now because their relationship had cooled in recent weeks.

I think this was news to Mario. While Ira was in the shower he called again. On hearing my voice he cut right through the small talk.

'Where are you sleeping?' he asked, with no preamble whatsoever.

'On the couch!' I answered, after the slightest of hesitations. The words hung in the air. The couch was a two-seater and we both knew that it would be impossible to sleep on it.

'Where is Ira?' he demanded. 'Put her on the phone!'

I could have been rude back, but I didn't see the point. I placed the receiver on the table and took my time about fetching Ira from the bathroom. It sounded like a hell of an argument, but Ira didn't seem too perturbed when she finally hung up. In fact, she took me to eat at Mario's main restaurant that night, just to show him that she didn't answer to him or anyone else. Mario was there, I said 'hello' when Ira pointed him out, but he ignored me completely and disappeared through the back. We had a loud and enjoyable meal and Mario didn't show his face again. He was getting angry though, and I was soon to discover just what that meant. While not one for direct confrontation, Mario was nevertheless perfectly able to deal with annoying foreigners hanging around his girlfriend.

The lay of the land became all too clear when I went to see Johan at the School Bar. I turned up in a suit and tie, all ready to negotiate. If I was going to put my life on the line, I was going to need good money. Sooner or later there was going to be trouble and my ability to fight, or lack of it, was going to be painfully exposed. I had accepted the inevitability of the situation and was hoping to get by on the bluff for a couple of weeks. Bouncers in Stockholm make good money so I had planned to save as much as I could in order to finance myself for a while. I decided that should a potential 'situation' arise I would give it my best shot and minimise the damage or the embarrassment in front of Ira. Not a very smart plan, but I was younger then and, as you have probably gathered, willing to take the occasional risk.

I could see from Johan's expression that things had changed since the previous occasion. He was cordial enough but the bottom line was that he was unable to offer me employment. It appeared that Mario had somehow found out the situation and had put a stop to it. He wouldn't say how Mario was able to exert such pressure but whatever threats he was using, Johan was opting for the quiet life.

'I'm sorry about all this, Barry,' he said, showing me towards the door.

'Yeah, I'm sorry too,' I sighed. I shook his hand and left. It seemed odd to me that anyone would be scared of a strange little chap like Mario, but there wasn't much I could do about it. In any case, I was confident that I would be able to secure less-demanding employment elsewhere and privately I was enormously relieved, for obvious reasons.

My confidence was ill-founded. Every time Ira lined me up with a job, Mario seemed to find out about it. All the bar managers had the same attitude as Johan when it came to employing me and I never found out why. All Ira could tell me was that the bloke 'had a lot of power' among the nightlife players in Stockholm. I ended up hating him. I was thoroughly enjoying myself in Sweden and he was doing a very good job of preventing me from earning a living there. After a couple of months I had to throw in the towel. I had spent nearly all of my money and was unable to earn more, so it was time, once again, to move on.

I didn't feel, however, like going back to the Canaries straight-away, so after racking my brains and talking it over with Ira, I decided to go to Holland.

# 11

# AMSTERDAM

There were a number of reasons why I chose Holland: it was only a day's journey by train for one thing, so I was able to get there without breaking the bank; the other, slightly more compelling reason, was that I would be able to visit Martja. I had kept in touch with the Dutch beauty since leaving Los Angeles and she had expressed an interest in seeing me again. Now was as good a time as any to make the trip, provided I made a determined effort to find employment straightaway in order to replenish my financial reserves.

As I said, I made the journey by train. The trip was uneventful except for an unpleasant moment when we crossed the German border. For some reason I hadn't expected there to be a checkpoint and I was sound asleep when the train pulled up. A Dutch guy who was sharing my carriage shook my arm to wake me up.

'It's the German border police,' he hissed. 'They're coming this way.' Still half asleep, I had a brief moment of panic. German border police? Jesus! The words triggered some deep-rooted fear in my psyche. In my semi-conscious state, reason seemed to be indicating that I had somehow travelled back in time fifty years to war-torn Europe. My hysteria increased considerably when a hand clamped on my shoulder and a German voice barked in my ear, 'Your papers please!'

'Oh Christ, no!' I yelled wildly, edging back into the corner of the compartment. I tripped over someone's feet and landed on a pile of suitcases. Scrabbling blindly, I managed to stand up but there was nowhere to run. The game was up and all I could do was stand there cowering, until I was arrested.

The Gestapo bully-boy, however, made no attempt to come after me. As I watched, rubbing my eyes, he mutated into a bemused-looking, modern day customs official.

'Sir, I am in a hurry even if you are not. Please would you be so kind as to let me see your passport?'

'Yeah, sure,' I mumbled, hurriedly proffering the required document. I could feel the combined stares of the other passengers burning into my neck as Fritz gave me back my passport and moved on.

'What was that all about?' asked my Dutch pal nervously. Not wanting to explain my embarrassingly racist reaction, I muttered some nonsense about having had a bad time of it in 'Nam and pretended to go back to sleep.

The journey took about twenty hours. When I finally staggered out of Centraal station and into the sunlight I was exhausted. Martja had given me the name of a cheap place to stay, as she didn't think her boyfriend would have agreed to having me at their house. I checked in at the Sleep Inn as soon as I found it and crashed out for the rest of the day.

After a shower and a change of clothes I felt revitalised and ready to explore. The hostel was, by any standards, pretty dire. It was, however, cheap, and that sealed the deal as far as I was concerned. I was going to have to stay there until I found myself a job.

Martja's mum and boyfriend were friendly enough. I spent quite a few nights at their house helping them test the quality of their home-grown. They also gave me some assistance in finding a job. I wanted to work in a gym and possessed some bogus references written for me by gym owners that I knew in the UK. The plan was to write to every gym in the Amsterdam yellow pages, enclosing copies of my references, and hope that at least one of them had a vacancy.

I wrote to over forty health establishments with no reply. Then one day, when I had just about given up hope, a letter was waiting for me at the reception of the Sleep Inn. The note invited me to call

a certain popular gymnasium near the Rembrantsplein to arrange a
meeting. I phoned immediately and was asked to turn up on Friday
at three o'clock. Finding the place was harder than I had
anticipated and I was a few minutes late. The owner met me at the
reception and ushered me inside.

'The ladies are already here,' he told me. 'Do you have your own
music? Or would you like to borrow a cassette from behind the
counter? I think you'll find we have plenty of suitable stuff to work
with.'

Ladies? Music? Cassettes? What on earth, I wondered, was the
lunatic gibbering on about? Then I was presented with a room full
of women in lycra who were quite obviously warming up for an
aerobics class, and the penny dropped. The man thought I was an
aerobics instructor and wanted me to start immediately.

Well, it came as a bit of a shock. Especially as I had no
experience or qualifications whatsoever in this particular field. I'd
never even watched an aerobics class before but I needed a job and
the way things were going I had to be grateful for any opportunity.

'Oh, I think I'll use one of your tapes. Something that they are
familiar with perhaps?' How hard could it be? I got changed into
my gym-wear, walked confidently to the front of the class, put the
tape in the stereo, and began. A couple of years ago, back in Spain,
I had lived with a girl who owned a Cindy Crawford workout video
that I occasionally leered at. I drew heavily on my memories of the
tape and applied some of my own personally acquired knowledge of
body mechanics.

In the end I got quite carried away, shouting things like, 'Work
that body!' and 'Stretch, 2-3-4-5-6-7-8.' How I kept it up for an
hour I'll never know, but when I finished I was pretty damn pleased
with myself. Aerobics was easy, I didn't know why I had ever been
so worried!

'See you next week, ladies,' I beamed at them, almost expecting
a round of applause. A couple of them glanced at me with half-
smiles as they filed out of the room but I put their lack of
enthusiasm down to their being in awe of their innovative new
aerobics mentor.

'What do you think?' I asked the owner after I'd changed. 'Have I got the job or what?'

'Er, well, you certainly have an interesting style,' he said with a masked expression. 'I tell you what, I'll talk it over with my partner and then we'll call you. OK?'

As you've probably guessed, the call never came. My brief foray into the world of aerobics instruction ended when I called the gym owner a few days later to see if he wanted to offer me a full-time position. He was guarded and noncommittal but I needed an answer and told him as much – which only served to prompt a scathing tirade. He let me know, in no uncertain terms, exactly just how bad my attempt had been.

'I don't know what kind of training they give you in England but it's obviously very substandard. I had to give everyone their money back. Aerobics instructor? Pah!' And with no further ceremony, he hung up.

It was a depressing time. I was genuinely slumming it for the first time in ages. With no money coming in I was forced to spend my nights at the Sleep Inn, watching telly with drop-outs from all over Europe. I couldn't even take Martja out for a drink. She had offered to pay but my pride wouldn't allow it. As far as I was concerned, a woman never paid on a date with me. This despite the fact that she was earning good money as the PA to the director of a blue chip company. Nowadays, of course, I have a lot more respect for women's lib – if they want to pay for their own drinks, I want to let them.

Eventually a solution was found – Martja knew someone who knew someone else who had an interest in a health club nearby. That person was prevailed upon to employ me on a temporary basis during my time in Holland. I worked as a body-building instructor, so while I didn't earn a fortune, I could at least go out and enjoy the city properly.

Martja really did a thorough job of showing me Amsterdam. The city is steeped in history, culture and heritage. We visited all the major attractions, but the place that had the biggest impact on me was the 'Achterhuis'.

The diary of a little Jewish girl in hiding during the Second World War has since sold millions of copies worldwide. I first read it at school and was equally horrified then. The Achterhuis, or Attic, is the actual converted loft where the Frank family lived during the Nazi occupation. Today it is a museum, preserved in as much authentic detail as possible from little Anne's day. There are many thought-provoking artefacts, not in the least original pages from the diary preserved in a glass case. The last room of the tour is the most chilling – a series of slide shows and displays records the evils of xenophobia and Fascism from the 1940s to the present day. On the way out of the building there's an option to make a donation to the Anti-Nazi League. I gave everything I had, and I wished I could have given more.

As for Martja, it was hard work trying to steal time alone together. She was living with her fella and, to be honest, was pretty much in love. I suppose I was an interesting diversion for her: a break from the routine. Either way her boyfriend, Dirk, was understandably more than a little perturbed by my inadequately explained presence in Amsterdam. Martja had apparently told him that she had hung about with an English guy after he had left LA, but I imagine she left out the part where we slept together. So Dirk was now wondering why I had suddenly turned up in Holland, and was voicing his objections to Martja. All of which was good news for me – it meant that in going out with me she was escaping the interrogations at home.

Not being a great lover of marijuana – in the lifestyle sense, as opposed to the occasional spliff – Amsterdam's famous coffee shops didn't hold a lot of appeal for me. The stuff just sends me to sleep. While I don't mind a smoke in my house at the end of a night out, I am averse to being semi-conscious when trying to enjoy an evening on the tiles. Like any good Dutch girl, Martja tried her best to convert me. She would drag me to The Bulldog or The Grasshopper raving about how a certain special blend of Lebanese Black, Red, whatever . . . would 'really put me on a buzz'. But the result was always the same: after a couple of tokes I would be slumped idiotically over the table with a stupid grin on my face while Martja shook her head in despair.

My favourite club was called It. Primarily a gay bar, it still let in proper blokes like me. Martja used to take me and a group of pals there to party of an evening. I am constantly shocked by the liberal-mindedness of the Dutch. For example, one night when I had decided to invest in an 'E' in order to enjoy a bit of a dance, I asked the dealer if she knew whether it was any good.

'Any good?' she frowned, 'Of course it's good. Why don't you go and test it in the machine if you don't trust me.'

I turned around and sure enough, the Dutch government had installed a machine in the club that would test the purity of any drugs bought on the premises. It was intended to stop citizens from buying Ecstasy with dangerous impurities – like rat poison – that we get in England. Such forward thinking has no doubt prevented many needless deaths in that splendid country.

I knew that things were going nowhere with Martja. She loved Dirk but she also enjoyed my company on the side. That was OK by me but it didn't half wind poor Dirk up. During one misguided attempt to rationalise her situation, Martja even talked me into coming round to their house for a meal. What a wake-up call that was. Whatever her original motivation, Martja's little soiree transformed Dirk for me from a talking point to a real person. I'd never even seen a photo of him before that night, which somehow made messing around with his girl much easier.

He tried to appear unconcerned and polite, but from the moment Martja introduced us I could sense his discomfort at my being in his house. In fact, I would even go as far as to call it downright hostility. He put on a good show of not being jealous but I could see right through him and then the strangest thing happened – I began to feel guilty. He was just a regular bloke trying to make a go of life. He had his flat, a business and a girl he cared about. He wasn't equipped to deal with competition like me. By the end of the evening I realised that I was little more than an intruder into a world I did not belong. Even before dessert arrived, I wanted to leave. I knew, with damning clarity, that it was time to go back to the Canaries. They had become my home and I had been away for too long.

# 12

# GRAN CANARIA II

Pete was pleased to hear that I was coming back to Tenerife. I was skint and so he arranged for Palm Springs to pay for my flight. When I got there I was already back on the photo team and moved me straight into the spare bedroom of his and Scarlet's luxurious duplex in Castle Harbour. Scarlet and I worked together again and after a month or so I was back on my feet financially.

There was now open hostility between Pete's security firm and the opposition. Because of this Pete liked to keep us all reasonably close by where he could keep an eye on us. It meant in practice that we all led pretty much sheltered lives, not mixing with anyone outside our own circle, but I didn't mind. I had been away from Pete and Scarlet for so long that I enjoyed the opportunity to spend time with them again.

The business of timeshare was getting more and more difficult in Tenerife, however, and after my initial thrill at being back I began to wonder where my real future lay.

Oh, don't worry, if there was one thing my travels had taught me, it was that the grass really is no greener on the other side of any proverbial fence. Happiness and satisfaction are commodities that cannot be sought geographically. They are there already, waiting to be discovered within. The flip side of that rather wise statement is that when you're at peace with yourself and the world, I truly believe there can be no greater privilege than having the financial security to be able to experience, first hand, the vast multitude of wonders and diversity that this planet has to offer.

This being my main and driving ambition in life, I had to start thinking about how to achieve it. Pete wanted me to go into business with him, running a modelling agency back in the UK. He would pony up the dough and I would manage the place. It would be easy money, he assured me, but I wasn't ready to brave the British climate again just yet.

Just when I was beginning to feel despondent about my lack of options, my old friend Jacky turned up out of the blue. And she had a job offer for me.

The Dreamlands Beach Club in Gran Canaria was a brand-new resort. They were going to be huge, and they wanted a photo team.

Jacky had already secured herself the position of manager, but told me that she would need a team captain. I accepted without hesitation and within two days I had left Pete and Scarlet behind in Tenerife and moved on to pastures new.

Looking back on events a month later, things had turned out very differently from my expectations. For a start the photo team was scrapped the day after I got there. Instead of letting this blow finish me off, however, I decided that it was as good a time as any to overcome my phobia of working on the street. I partnered up with Jacky and surprised myself at how good I actually was. I made new friends and learned to interact once more in a community where I wasn't constantly in Pete's shadow. As much as I loved the bloke, I found that my status as a mate of his affected everyone's attitude towards me while I was living in Tenerife. Over in Gran Canaria he didn't even come into the picture.

Because most of the OPCs were old hands and had been around the business for ages, practical jokes and wind-ups were rife – one of the most annoying of which was when your car got 'done'. Most OPCs would prefer to drive their couples to the resort in their hire cars instead of taking the free taxi because they wouldn't then be stranded after dropping the couple off at the reception. With the hot weather, it was normal to leave your vehicle unlocked, with the windows down, in order to prevent the temperature inside surpassing that of the main chamber in Hell. If you were foolish enough to leave your car unattended like this round other OPCs then you were fair game.

It always seemed to happen to me when I had a couple I needed to drive to the resort. Couples were sometimes hesitant to get into the car of a stranger and it didn't help matters much when I turned the ignition key, and the radiator along with the stereo and windscreen wipers (which had been pulled out of their regular position) all came on at full power. The indicator and headlights would also come on and the horn would be hanging loose. The horn was particularly annoying because, when trying to clip it back into place, it would continue sounding, above and beyond the noise of everything else. You can imagine what fun it was trying to keep the couple sweet while you dealt with the mayhem.

There were plenty of lesser traps to fall into. If you gave someone a drink of your Coke you had to check it when you got it back. A few slits made in the neck of the bottle with a pocket knife would ensure that you spilt it all down your top the next time you had a swig. My personal favourite was the old 'being-rude-to-passers-by-in-such-a-way-that-your-mate-got-the-blame' lark. For example, if your pal was drinking from a bottle of water while a large-breasted girl was walking past, you would shout, 'Hey, big tits! Do you want some of my water?' and quickly look the other way before she swung round and tore into your pal. The best incident of this to date is when a couple of my mates were on holiday in Birmingham. Jimmy is a white bloke and Junior is black, and they were larking about on their way into a football match. On seeing a policeman, Junior ran up to him complaining that Jimmy had been following him around all day and could the copper make him stop? The copper had seen it all before and wasn't interested.

'Piss off, why don't you, before you get a clip round the lughole!' was his advice.

Deflated, Junior started walking back to Jimmy but as the officer turned away, Jimmy put on his best Jamaican accent, 'Focking blood clatt, Babylan!' he spat loudly after the retreating lawman. The copper was furious. He wheeled round on Junior, eyes full of fury.

'What did you say?' he bawled. 'Do you think you're fucking clever?' Junior tried helplessly to assert his innocence through body language but it was a lost cause. The policeman had heard a Jamaican accent and had immediately connected it to the black youth behind him. He began pushing through the crowd towards Junior who had to leg it back up the tunnel and missed the game completely.

All the piss-taking did sometimes get out of hand. There weren't many fights because, after all, we lived on a small island and no-one would have benefitted from friction within the team. There was one bloke who I nearly came to blows with a few times though, and his name was Mark. Mark was a Scouser and he used to suffer a lot from small man's complex. Being only 4ft 11in. he constantly felt the need to prove himself. He ruthlessly took the piss out of others but couldn't really take it when the tables were turned. The trouble was that he used to say things that left him wide open to abuse. I remember one day at breakfast when he mentioned to me that he had six brothers, all the same size as him. I casually enquired as to whether their names were Sleepy, Dopey, Doc, etc., and he flew off the handle.

One day, I forget the exact reason why, things came to a head. We were squared up to each other and it looked like it was going to kick off, when I had the bright idea of settling it in the boxing ring. He accepted my challenge and we set the date for the following Friday.

It wasn't supposed to be a big deal but somehow word got round and it was all anyone could talk about for the rest of the week. Puerto Rico divided into two camps, his and mine. There were huge wagers being laid and, to protect their interests, my supporters insisted on training me. My brother was in Gran Canaria as well by this time and he and his pals hired a car so that they could drive in front of me during my training runs. They sang Rocky songs at me and encouraged me to shadow box as I ran. Even back at the apartment there was still no rest. As soon as I put my feet up my pal Paul would be banging at the door carrying focus mits and pads. More than once I cursed myself for letting the whole thing get started in the first place. The good news was that as far as my spies could gather, Mark was doing no training at all. Apparently he thought that his natural aggression was going to be the deciding factor.

Friday rolled round with astonishing speed and at lunchtime we all set off to the gym in Arguineguin, where they had given us permission to stage our bout. I was pretty nervous because of the sheer volume of people who had turned out to watch. There was a convoy of about 70 cars all following us as we drove down to the gym. Clint and Jimmy, our street captains, were begging us to get it over with as quickly as possible because absolutely everyone had come down to watch. No work was being done for the other companies either, such was the appeal of the event.

We all packed into the gym and there was a space created in the middle for Mark and myself. Jimmy was to referee and, despite my butterflies, I was quietly confident that I would be victorious. I had the advantage in size, strength and fitness, and there was no way I was going to give up. Not in front of this lot, any road.

Jimmy called for silence, we touched gloves and off we went. We both charged in like madmen. I caught him with a cracking left and knocked his headguard off. He instinctively ducked his head to cover up and, smelling blood, I steamed in for an uppercut. Unluckily for me, Mark chose that precise moment to bob back up. The back of his head crunched into my nose and blood started jetting out. The fight was stopped momentarily while the damage was assessed and Jimmy declared me unfit to carry on.

'Hang on!' I said. 'I'll be alright in a minute when the bleeding stops!'

'Baz, just go and look at yourself in the mirror,' he told me. Why, I wondered? It was just a nose bleed, it didn't hurt all that much. Still, I humoured him by going into the changing rooms for a look.

I tell you what, when I saw the damage in the mirror it soon started to hurt! My conk was swollen up like a football. And the whole thing had moved an inch to the left. It was well and truly broken and there was no way I was going to be able to continue.

159

Gutted, I went back into the hall to announce my decision. Mark let out a shriek of joy and threw his gloves in the air. He was claiming victory on the grounds of a technical knockout and so were his supporters. I challenged him to a rematch a couple of weeks later but he took the opportunity to announce his retirement, undefeated, from the world of boxing. From that day to this I have not been able to get him back in the ring.

Meanwhile there were changes afoot at the Dreamlands Beach Club. Up until now the companies in Gran Canaria had managed without the need for clumpers. The timeshare resorts ran pretty smoothly without having to threaten their OPCs with violence and, on the whole, it made for a far more pleasant working environment. Pete, however, was of the opinion that this had been going on for quite long enough. And so, without warning, he flew over and turned up at one of our pay meetings. He sat and had a drink with me until one of the big bosses turned up and then nipped off to have a word with him in private. When he came back he didn't tell me about the conversation, just that I would be 'seeing a lot more of him from now on'.

Sure enough, a couple of days later, it was announced in the morning meeting that Dreamlands now had clumpers. We were told not to worry and that anyone who wanted to leave would be allowed to do so. All this may have fooled the new OPCs but those of us who had been around a bit knew better. There was no way that Dreamlands was going to pay clumpers without using them. The good OPCs were going to be trapped and that was that. The problem was if our company was paying clumpers then the rest would follow suit inside of a week anyway, so it was very much a case of better the devil you knew.

None of these developments really applied to me. Pete was my mate and wouldn't stop me from working where I wanted, so I welcomed the fact that he was going to be visiting more often.

Soon all the timeshares on the island were paying protection money to Pete and he was raking it in nicely. He was coming over about once every two weeks and Scarlet was coming with him. The downside with Pete's sort of business is the stress. The rival firms in Tenerife were constantly testing his resolve and regular violence ensued. I won't go into detail, partly because it's not my story, but suffice to say that it was all most unpleasant. After a while the strain of it all became too much for Scarlet who was still only twenty at this stage. They split up and Scarlet came over to live with me in Gran Canaria. This suited Pete because he knew that I would keep an eye on her and he could still pop over and see her every so often.

We were a nice little posse. Scarlet, my brother and me. For a while everything was rosy. We were all doing well at work except for the occasional problem with the receptionists. You see, I was still a terrible blagger and the head receptionist had a bit of a vendetta against me. All my couples were subjected to extreme scrutiny when they got to reception to make sure that they were the right age, owned their own home etc. Sometimes this would annoy the couple so much that they would bolt before I was paid. I accepted this as the price to pay for the blags that I did get away with. The problem was that I now had my brother and Scarlet to think about. They were both working on my number and were losing too much money at the hands of the receptionist. Eventually, my brother and Scarlet collared me and demanded that I do something about it.

'Like what?' I pleaded. But they were ready. They told me that I had to make friends with the head reception girl and make her better disposed towards me. They even found out where she went drinking so that I could 'accidentally' bump into her while I was out.

I did what I was supposed to and in the course of befriending her we played a few games of pool. We had a couple of drinks and shot the breeze. After an hour or so I felt that I had done enough. I started to make my excuses and got up to leave, mentioning that I wanted to have a look round some of the other bars. To my shock she announced that she would like to come with me.

'Where are we going then?' she asked, knocking back her drink and slipping her hand into mine. My eyes narrowed and I realised that perhaps I might have turned on the charm a little too much. This woman was now intent on sleeping with me. Normally I would have been more than obliging but this lady was in her fifties and married to one of Dreamlands' executives. In a dilemma, I took her to a quiet bar so that no-one would see us. Unfortunately she took this to mean that I wanted to start necking. I did the only thing I could do in such a situation. I got drunk.

After half an hour's squelching at the back of the bar, during which I set records for rapid consumption of Jack Daniels, I told my companion that I was tired and would need to be heading home soon – now, in fact! I chirpily threw my keys in the air and caught them before making one last attempt to escape.

No such luck. Even before I got out of the bar I could hear the clacking of her high heels as she ran to catch me up.

'You couldn't drop me off, could you?' she leered. 'It's on your way.'

I knew that I was clean out of options. I drove her to her villa and when I stopped to let her out she pounced. Right there on the back seat of my car, with her husband and kids asleep inside the house, I did the deed.

The next morning I told my brother and Scarlet just how far I had gone to protect their wage packets. Far from being sympathetic, they found it hilarious. Scarlet was all for me bringing the woman home and doing it again so that we could secretly video the event and use it to blackmail her. Thankfully, such lengths were to prove unnecessary – from that moment on, all the couples on my number passed through reception without a hitch.

I couldn't have known it at the time but a chapter of my life was about to close forever. One morning Scarlet and I were on our way to the OPC meeting when my street captain and good friend, Jimmy Gall, pulled me to one side. His expression unfathomable, he sat me on a wall, took a deep breath and looked straight at me.

'I don't know how to tell you this, Barry,' he said quietly. 'Pete is dead.'

'Dead?' I said blankly. 'What do you mean?'

'He was shot last night in Tenerife. The rest I don't know. I just thought you and Scarlet might need some time off work, that's all.'

It didn't sink in for a good while. I quickly found Scarlet and we drove around for the entire day in a daze. The magnitude of what had happened somehow preventing us from reacting. Pete had always maintained that he would die young and now he had. That night Scarlet and I just lay in each other's arms, not sleeping. The tears didn't come until the project director of Dreamlands summoned us to his office the next day. He offered condolences and said that if we wanted financial help to go back for the funeral then Dreamlands would pay. That man's kindness seemed to act as a trigger for our emotions and, without warning, our tears burst forth. Scarlet and I rocked each other back and forth and cried and cried.

Eventually we pieced together what had happened. Pete had been acting strangely for some time. Scarlet and I caught him crying during a shopping trip for no apparent reason. Additionally, some of his clumpers had commented that he was acting irrationally – talking about having an 'Old Chicago'-style war with some of his rivals.

We thought that he might need a bit of a rest and Scarlet had convinced him to go and see a psychiatrist the next time he was in England. We kept an eye on him but noticed no further signs of stress so we pretty much forgot about it.

It was a few weeks later when he summoned a couple of his men for what was supposed to be a standard case of putting the frighteners on a clumper who worked for another firm. As far as Pete's men knew, they were just going along for back-up while Pete had a word in the bloke's ear – nothing serious, just intimidate him a little and then leave.

Pete had other ideas. To everyone's horror, as soon as he entered the apartment he pulled out a huge knife and went for the rival clumper, to the horror of the clumper's friend in the apartment with him. Even as he lunged, one of his own henchmen tried to stop him.

'Pete, what are you doing? I thought you were just going to give him a talking to,' he pleaded, attempting to block Pete's way. Pete's eyes flashed.

'You're either with me or you're against me!' he raged. And with that he tore into one of his own men, stabbing his henchman repeatedly in the torso. The clumper's friend on seeing this, jumped over the first-floor balcony. He escaped but broke his leg in the process. Meanwhile, the actual chap that Pete was after was naturally more than a little worried. As a last resort he pulled out a gun, which he later claimed he was looking after for a friend, and shot Pete once. Once was all it took and Pete died before he reached the hospital.

Pete's death affected Scarlet and me in different ways. Scarlet went off the rails on an extended drinking binge. It was the most unhappy I had ever seen her and I was powerless to help. I went the other way. I withdrew into myself and, unable to deal with friends and family, I threw all my energy into work.

The community we lived in really did rally round us. Well-wishers called in at the flat and people went out of their way to help and understand. Eventually the pain dulled to a manageable level and life began to assume a semblance of order once more. There are times even now when I hear Pete's name mentioned in conversation, or when I come across an old photo, that the world stops all over again.

I had been keeping in touch with Ira since getting back to the Canaries and she had decided, to my delight, to come and live in Gran Canaria. She was going to work for a rival company as an OPC. She would be getting free accommodation and flights as was the norm and would be living in the next town. Scarlet and I went to pick her up from the airport and even Scarlet, no slouch herself, had to admit that she was stunning. Her hair was bobbed and stylish, her nails long and elegant and her smile inviting.

We all went out that night and became fast friends. Pretty soon I was seeing Ira and we moved in together, although with hindsight I wish that we had just remained friends. We had such a chaotic relationship that it ended up being more hassle than it was worth. One day we would be all over one another and the next day we would be hurling household appliances at each other. By household appliances I literally mean televisions, irons and stereos. Although I have to admit that it was Ira who did most of the hurling. For a girl, she can't half lob stuff.

Needing, for safety reasons, to get out of the house in the evenings, I came up with a new idea for a business. The 'pub crawl' had been done in Tenerife before, but not to my knowledge in Gran Canaria. The 'pub crawl' took the form of a party of tourists who I would lead round five bars. It took place once a week and was pretty easy to organise. I had cheap ticket books photocopied and distributed to the OPCs who sold them for me. The tickets cost seven pounds fifty per person. Five pounds of this was paid direct to the seller as deposit. The seller then kept this fiver as his commission. The balance of two pounds fifty a head was paid to me on the door. For this, the punter got one free drink in each bar (paid for by the bar owner) and an organised party game. The DJ in each bar took care of the party game, so after I had taken the door money there was nothing left for me to do except lead the party to the next pub at the end of each allotted hour. Also, the owner of each bar paid me fifty pence per head to keep the pub group in his bar for the hour. So, for example, from a pub crawl of one hundred people I made five hundred pounds. My overheads were in the region of fifteen pounds per week so it was nearly all profit.

I split the pub crawl with my brother and continued OPCing during the week. The night of the pub crawl was Friday and we looked forward to it with a passion. For a start, it was like working in a sweet shop. The girls were all over us just because they thought we were flash working there. We didn't even have to try very hard to pull. They chatted us up, and we let them! We got free drinks too as part of the deal negotiated with the bar owners. The only fly in the ointment was that sometimes punters would realise that they had been ripped off and start demanding their money back. At first my brother and I used to blame each other when this happened. I would send whingers over to him and vice versa but we soon realised that this was only a short-term solution. After a while we invented a character called 'Big Freddy' who was the boss. Whenever anyone complained after that we told them to see Freddy when he came down later, as we were little more than a couple of paid flunkies.

Most times this would work and the punter's anger would be redirected towards the mysterious Freddy, but not always. Sometimes customers could get really insistent about wanting their money back. If we were unable to calm a customer down a crowd would start to form. Pretty soon everyone would be on our case demanding compensation. My brother and I had an agreement not to give the money back under any circumstances, so when we found ourselves faced with this situation, all we could do was – somewhat blatantly – turn tail and run. Many's the time we've pounded hell for leather towards the car with an angry lynch mob only seconds behind us – but on the whole it was worth it. We had invented a way of going out on a Friday night, getting free drinks, guaranteed sex and two hundred and fifty quid each into the bargain.

We started the pub crawl during one of the periods that Ira and I were separated. Ira soon started attending the pub crawl to 'help out'. She distributed free drinks in the meeting point bar and growled at any girls who flirted with me. I found it funny. The rumours she had heard about the easy women at those crawls had sparked something in her. I was happy enough, though, and for a short time we got on really well again.

It didn't last. We were obviously not destined to be together and after a while we were back at each other's throats. It occurred to me that we were getting stuck in a rut. Every time we split up and tried to move forward we ended up back together and reliving the same old painful routines.

Eventually, I realised that I would have to take drastic action for both our sakes. That opportunity arose when an old mate of mine approached me with the offer of a manager's job for a new photo team back in Tenerife. The company was called The Sun Club and had a good reputation so I took the chance and broke the loop.

# 13

# TENERIFE V

I drove over to Tenerife in a convoy with some of my friends who were also returning to work there. It involved a long drive to the North of the island and a four hour ferry ride to Puerto de la Cruz before another long drive down to the south of Tenerife. It would have been a lot cheaper and easier to fly but we chose to take cars because we had all accumulated so much stuff during our stint in GC. It was quite a trek but worth it when we got there. For the first time ever in company accommodation I was able to enjoy a decent standard of living, thanks to my television and video as well as all the other mod cons I had brought with me.

I was working for a different company from my fellow travellers so I was unable to share a house with them, but I ended up living with a girl called Laura who was a mate of mine anyway. She and I were working together, trying to set up the new photo team for The Sun Club.

The wage structure we were offered by our new boss was healthy enough but I was soon to discover that photo team management was no longer the golden goose of yore. These days every street OPC was using trick scratch cards to get their couples in. These worked by making the punter think that they had won an expensive prize, like five hundred quid in cash. In reality they had only won a cheap watch. Clever wording on the card helped the company avoid actually paying out any money when a couple handed in their winning ticket. You could tell which were the 'winning' tickets by a tiny but discernible distinguishing mark that wasn't on the other cards. You made sure that you gave everybody in a particular family losing cards except for, perhaps, their little girl, to whom you would give a winner. Gone was the necessity to talk to your couple for ages about the wonderful benefits of your resort. If you could persuade a family to take your scratch cards, all you had to do was put on a convincing performance of being amazed when they won their predestined 'five hundred quid'. It was a direct appeal to their greed and the whole pitch took less than five minutes. If the couple believed you, they came, simple as that. Today you can't get away with such blatant trickery but you could back then and it didn't half make the job easier. So it was an uphill struggle trying to convince the veteran street OPCs to give up their evenings for the extended rigmarole of photo pitching. We tried, obviously, but all we ended up with was a team of people who had failed on the street. The same character traits that had made them street OPC failures also, quite predictably, let them down on the photo team. My override as a photo manager was a pittance, so I had to work during the day to supplement my income.

In the meantime, after one month the company housing ran out and I moved into a lovely house in the village of Adeje. I shared with two brothers and one of their girlfriends – the party with whom I had driven over the previous month, and who are some of the nicest people I have met since starting in the business. We took up all kinds of wholesome activities, like walks in the mountains and home-cooked meals. They were decent folk so I tried to follow their example. For the most part I succeeded. The one lapse I did have put me well and truly in the dog-house for several days. It's funny – you can conduct yourself impeccably for weeks on end and no-one seems to notice, but the one time your flatmates return unexpectedly early from a weekend away and catch you enjoying a cocaine-fuelled, three-in-a-bed sex session with an ex- girlfriend and a young waitress, they never let you forget it . . .

My old pal Luis still owned the studio that we used for the photo team. He was getting paid a fair amount by The Sun Club and he kept me sweet by teaching me to surf on our days off. He was also extremely generous with the Charlie. Even I was surprised at how much of that stuff was being used by my new colleagues and I actually found myself turning down the occasional line. Not too often, obviously. That would have been rude.

The island seemed to have changed. I couldn't put my finger on it exactly, but to my mind a lot of the vitality had drained away when the old characters left the place. Most of the guys that I had OPC'd with in the early days had moved on to different islands and even different countries. Many of them were now running teams of their own. Some of the more ambitious had even reached the dizzy heights of resort management, which is the topmost branch of the tree, home only to investors and money men. Thankfully there were still one or two faces left. Mad Tony, for example, was becoming part of the island's folklore.

Tony was a young fellow from the south of England and he was, well, different from everyone else. It was as though insanity was woven deeply into the fabric of his very being – although he was travelling through life in the same direction as the rest of us, it seemed to be always by a slightly different route. When pitching couples he had a vast array of madcap intros that could only work for him. Their very oddness was guaranteed to stop a couple in their tracks.

'Speaking the Queen's and full of beans?'

'What's the matter chief? Flip-flops on fire?'

'You're a winner, I'm a winner. Everyone's a chicken dinner!'

'SQUEAL the brakes on governor!'

'No timeshares, deckchairs or armchairs luvvy!'

And the old classic when a couple was expressing doubts about the authenticity of the winning scratch card, 'Shut it muppet! Are you calling me a liar?'

Oh yes, he had a line for every occasion did Tony. But that was by no means the extent of his entertainment value. What most of us loved about him was his propensity for getting into awkward situations, generally the kind that could happen to anybody, but they didn't, they always happened to Tony.

One time Tony was at the reception checking in a couple and he had left his baseball cap outside on a bench. Someone (God knows why) had a dead budgie, and saw fit to leave it in Tony's hat for a joke. Not a particularly funny one, just one of those little diversions that can sometimes see us through an otherwise dull morning. The stakes were raised when Tony returned from the reception area and failed to notice the green and yellow cadaver in his hat. He just lobbed it onto his head, pulled the peak to the front and drove off on his scooter. All morning he rode around with the bird sticking out of the hole in the back of his hat. People stared curiously but he remained oblivious. Then, on his way home for lunch, he noticed that the police were by the side of the road up ahead. They sometimes did spot checks on vehicles to make sure that the insurance was up to date, that kind of thing. Tony remembered that he was wearing a baseball cap with his company logo emblazoned on the front, and knowing how much the police hated OPCs, decided to quickly whip it back to front. He didn't want to draw unnecessary attention to himself, after all.

With an ingratiating smile he tried to ride straight past. Of course, all the police saw was some lunatic with a parrot on his head driving past laughing at them. They pulled him over immediately and gave him a good kicking. The worst part for Tony must have been wondering where on earth the bird had come from in the first place.

People like Tony made my time in Tenerife more bearable but really, all I was doing was biding my time away from Ira to make sure I was genuinely over her. I didn't want to get stuck in the same old rut when I went back to GC. All the same, I would have returned a lot sooner if it wasn't for my flatmates: Rupert, Eddy and Deedee. Another mate of ours moved in, Jasper was his name, and we became proper drinking buddies.

It wasn't so much the amount of alcohol we drank that made our sessions memorable, it was the way it affected our reasoning and common sense. One night we discovered that we had both learned judo as teenagers and an argument ensued as to who was the best. The discussion escalated until we ended up driving to a deserted beach with five car loads of our pals. A circle was drawn on the sand

and at three o'clock in the morning, by the light of the car headlamps, we had it out. To my chagrin, he was actually better than me – though I wouldn't mind another go when we're both sober sometime.

Throughout my self-imposed exile in Tenerife I was regularly keeping in contact with my mates in Gran Canaria and, eventually, I heard the news that I had been waiting for. Ira had a new boyfriend. He was in his late thirties, a slender, balding chap from Pakistan called Gunter, and, what's more, she was having his baby. While I had mixed feelings about this information, it did mean that I could finally go back home. With Ira safely tied up in a long-term relationship I wouldn't have to be on my guard about getting mixed up with her again. I made the necessary phone calls and in no time at all I was on my way back to Gran Canaria.

# 14

# GRAN CANARIA III

My triumphant return was marred by the fact that I was absolutely broke. Everyone took the piss about me being the only person to get an OPC manager's job and end up worse off than when I started. It didn't last long though – I chose a good company and got my head down during my month's free accommodation. Soon I was flush and sharing a nice villa with a couple of good mates.

I was doing well enough OPCing but after so many years in the business I began to wonder if there wasn't an easier way of maintaining my standard of living. One day it hit me. The answer had been there all along. Why didn't I just do the pub crawl full time? Less work, more money and a whole lot more fun. I liked having a partner for these sort of projects, so I went to see Jimmy Gall. Jimmy had just been laid off by Dreamlands after many years, loyal service and was understandably down in the dumps. He went for the idea with as much enthusiasm as me and a day later we were in business.

We made a couple of changes to the basic set-up of the operation that my brother and I used to run. For a start, we sold a good amount of tickets ourselves. We put a lot more effort into making sure that everyone else was selling too and soon we had enough punters for two pub crawls a week. The other change was that we made the games ruder. I no longer left the entertainment in the hands of the DJ, preferring to get behind the mike myself. You wouldn't believe the things young Brits will do on holiday – as part of the games I would have people naked on stage, girls snogging each other, people indulging in oral and even full sex in a normal bar.

It was my idea of heaven. I had told Jimmy to expect plenty of female attention but he still wasn't fully prepared.

'Christ, it's like being a rock star!' he grinned out of the corner of his mouth as a couple of young hopefuls slipped their hands down his trousers. The girls we knew got in on the act too and often came along to prey on the young male tourists.

We would buy a few cheap bottles of champagne to give away as prizes and pretty soon complaints became a thing of the past. Every one of our punters enjoyed a boisterous night out. People would come up to us all evening to tell us what a great time they were having. We could do no wrong. We were making about eight hundred quid a week each tax free, and were thoroughly enjoying ourselves .

We became so blasé about the easy sex that we didn't care about getting caught two-timing girls that we were seeing. What the hell was the general attitude. After all, there were plenty more where they came from. On one occasion I was in the DJ booth enjoying a demonstration of 'pink oboe skills' from a girl who had won a bottle of champagne in a previous competition when I looked up and saw the girl that I was supposed to be with marching through the crowd towards me. Being flash, I tried to leave it until the last possible second before withdrawing but predictably, I got busted. Even then I managed to talk my way out of it.

'Cor, stop it will you,' I tutted at the young lady on her knees. 'Crazy isn't she?' I said by way of comment to my girlfriend as I shook my head, rolled my eyes skyward and announced the next record.

Jimmy and I became legends among the OPC community. Everyone wanted to hear about our escapades on the pub crawls and maybe ogle some of the photos that I had managed to persuade the previous night's beauty to pose for. It was the life of Riley and, for a while at least, it was only going to get better.

We had been running the pub crawls for several months when

Jimmy got offered the job of team captain for a small company in the next town. He asked me if I wanted to share it with him and I readily agreed. As long as it didn't interfere with the running of the pub crawls then I was game. It even meant that we could photocopy the ticket books for free in the company's marketing office.

It was a very small company and as we didn't really need the job, Jimmy and I were able to negotiate an excellent salary deal. For running a five-or-six man team we were being paid about four hundred quid a week each plus having our mobile phone bills taken care of. The team practically ran itself so we had as much free time as before.

In the daytimes I got settled into a nice little routine. We would have breakfast at nine o'clock while we took the morning meeting in a little bar, then we'd head off to my complex for a few games of chess by the pool. After which I liked to get oiled-up with suntan lotion and spend the rest of the day floating round the pool on my lilo. Occasionally, the boss would ring up to ask if everyone was working hard and I would reply that they were indeed and then cut him off, claiming that I had to go and help someone to close a couple. That's the beauty of mobile phones, your boss has no idea where you are when he phones you.

Of course, that works both ways. When your boss phones you on his mobile, you similarly have no idea where he might be calling from either. On one occasion he caught me bang-to-rights. I was gently drifting round my swimming pool enjoying the glorious afternoon sun when the shrilling of the telephone interrupted my peaceful reverie.

'Hello, Shaun,' I identified him from the screen. 'Everything all right?'

'Yes,' said my boss, 'it's just that we are having a bit of a slow day and I wanted to make sure that you were all still working hard.'

'Oh yes! Grafting like Trojans!' I replied, giving myself the gentlest of shoves off the side of the pool with my big toe. My fridge was on an extension cord across the way and with practised ease I directed my lilo towards it so that I could reach in for a beer. 'I'm going to have to call you back Shaun. Lee is struggling with a couple and he needs my help to close them.' I was just about to cut him off when he calmly accused me of being a lying bastard. That shocked me a bit so I asked him what he meant.

'Well, Barry, I am at this moment observing you from over your swimming pool wall. If you look up you'll see me.' I looked up dumbly and waved. He waved back. Desperately I tried to recover.

'You can't go creeping up on people like that,' I said. 'It's just downright sneaky!'

'Sneaky. That's a good word,' he mused. 'I tell you what, why don't you SNEAK back to work and see if you can SNEAK a few couples in this afternoon. That way I might not have to SNEAK into my boss's office in the morning and explain to him the real reason why we had a bad day today.'

On the whole Shaun gave us an easy ride. As long as the team was performing he didn't care too much what Jimmy and I did with our afternoons. For the next couple of years, Jimmy and I had a great time of it. The only threat to our existence came when our pub crawl photographer tried to sell us out to a major English Sunday tabloid.

It had always been a worry at the back of my mind that some insanely jealous young lad would try to sell the story. It had all the ingredients: sun, sangria, sex and the added bonus that a lot of the drinkers were under eighteen. Most of the Brit-workers were a decent bunch and you could trust them not to grass, but this little fella was a heroin addict and I suppose he must have been hard up. That didn't make me any happier about it at the time and I chased him around with a baseball bat for about a week.

The first sign of trouble was when our secretary rang me up one morning to say that there had been two reporters looking for me down at the reception of the timeshare. Then OPCs from other companies started phoning me to say that there were a couple of people going round asking questions about the pub crawl. No one spoke to them but, by asking around, I soon discovered that it was Scottish Dave, the photographer, who had grassed me up to them. All very worrying because the man had literally hundreds of incriminating photos of people up to no good on our pub crawl.

I had to think fast. The first thing I did was to ring every street captain in Puerto Rico and ask him to tell his OPCs not to talk to any strange middle-aged couples about the pub crawl. Then I went round all the bars and made sure everyone there knew not to talk to them. All in, I think I did a pretty good job of shutting the whole thing up. The next objective was to locate Dave and force him to make a retraction. I grabbed one of my mates and a baseball bat and we went looking. The little bastard seemed to be blessed with the luck of the devil and for a week he stayed one jump ahead of us. Then we heard that he had escaped and gone back to Edinburgh so we had to abandon the chase.

I never spoke to those reporters but two weeks later another one turned up at the beginning of a pub crawl and asked for our comments. We had to think fast but managed to convince him that there wasn't a story worth printing. We made a big show of asking people their age when they turned up at the door, and refused admission to anyone who looked under the age of eighteen. We talked about Dave's heroin problem and what a shame it was that he had to resort to such lengths to try and earn a crust. The hack pulled out a load of compromising photos. Most of them were of me taken during the sex games on stage in one of the bars. Some of them left nothing at all to the imagination. We laughed it off, telling him that those particular photos were nothing to do with the pub crawl at all and were in fact from a particularly bawdy stag night at our friend's recent wedding. We gave him a free ticket and invited him to come along and judge for himself exactly how outrageous we were. Then we dragged him around with us for what we made sure was the tamest pub crawl ever. The games were musical chairs and yard of ale competitions. The usual nerdy office night out stuff. Within an hour the reporter was bored stiff. So wherever you are Dave, better luck next time old chum!

Jimmy had a nephew called Fred. He wanted to come over to Gran Canaria and work so we gave him a job OPCing for our company and I ended up sharing a gaff with him. He was a great laugh and I spent a lot of time with him. One of his best traits was that he always seemed to owe me money and he was quite happy to work it off by way of 'dares'.

One time he owed me about twenty quid and the deal was, to clear the debt, that he had to stomp into the pub across the road wearing only my judo suit and no shoes. Avoiding making eye contact with anyone, he had to march straight up to the bar and order a double whisky. Whenever anyone asked him what he was up to he had to reply that the 'voices' had told him that it was time to avenge his brother's death . . . He wasn't allowed to smile during this performance or the dare was void.

When he owed more money the stakes went up. Some girl had left a black bra under one of our beds and for a larger amount of money Fred would have to wear this under a very thin see-through shirt and go into town for a drink, looking all the time like some kind of weirdo who liked wearing women's underwear. When anyone asked him why he had a bra on, he was only allowed to respond by looking embarrassed and denying it till he was blue in the face.

Jimmy and I both knew that our run of good luck couldn't last forever and after nearly two years of being paid for virtually nothing, the first cracks started appearing in the woodwork. The timeshare company we were working for finally woke up to the fact that it was losing copious amounts of money each week and decided to close down. The only thing we could do was sell the team to a rival company, so we brokered a deal and concentrated on the pub crawls.

The next half of the double whammy was to arrive a couple of weeks later while Jimmy was on holiday. One of the most powerful timeshare barons on the island had got wind that his OPCs were selling tickets for the pub crawl during working hours and he was very angry about it. The upshot of it all was that I had to leave the island in a hurry or pay a serious fine. There was, as always, the third option of severe personal harm but I chose not to dwell on that. Having no savings, as usual, I had no option but to skidaddle. – I was in England in less than twelve hours.

# 15

# MEXICO

As you can imagine, it was a bit of a culture shock for me. In two weeks I'd gone from being on top of the world, earning good money from two jobs and living the high life on a sub-tropical island to being skint in England with nowhere to go.

For a while Jase and I started planning a trip around America. He secured me some well-paid work as a welder at his rally firm – despite the fact that I'd never welded anything in my life. I did pick up bits and pieces while I was there but I wouldn't say they got their money's worth. I managed to save over a grand in two weeks and entrusted this to Jason's bank account for safe-keeping. The America trip had to be shelved when my visa application was refused. We had a think about it and decided that Mexico would be just as good. Scarlet, who was at a loose end, said that she would like to come too.

We all met up in Coventry one day for a drink and to discuss the coming adventure. We were all going to be flying out on separate flights so that we could get cheap last-minute deals.

Jason had my money in an envelope and he handed it over to me when we met. I tucked it away in my jacket pocket as we entered the first bar. We were drinking heavily and the mood was buoyant. Amid the joviality, Jason asked me to make sure that the money was still safely nestled in my pocket. Absent-mindedly, I patted its location to make sure, and the bottom fell out of my world. It had gone. It was the sum total of my financial worth and I had lost it. I already knew as we ran round the pubs looking underneath the seats that we wouldn't find the envelope. Eleven hundred quid had gone up in smoke, which meant that I was totally broke. I could no longer go to Mexico, or anywhere else for that matter. Not knowing how to react, I didn't react at all. It was all to come out at a later date, but for now I made light of it, finished my drink and went home.

Over the next few days I racked my brains for a quick money-making scheme and the best I could come up with was to buy one thousand pounds worth of forged banknotes from some contacts I knew and get them changed in small shops. An opportunity to buy some materialised a few days later but my Dad put a stop to all that nonsense by lending me the money instead.

I was flying out ahead of the other two. Central America promised to be very different to anywhere else I had ever been, and was also much further away. There was obvious trepidation mixed with my excitement, and also some pressure. This was the first time I'd gone into debt to finance my travelling and I didn't like it. It was essential that I get a job as soon as possible so that I could pay my Dad back and get on with enjoying the experience.

I flew from Heathrow on a flight which took about fourteen hours. It was daylight when we began our final descent into Cancun airport and I was able to get a good look out of the window as we neared our destination.

Imagine a giant, dark green carpet stretching out to the horizon in every direction but one. This last edge of the forest backing right up to the whitest beach you've ever seen, which in turn gave way to the lightest blue sea. I had read that Cancun had been selected by tourist development computers as perhaps the most desirable place in Mexico to develop a new resort and I have to say that from my viewpoint in the sky at least, I couldn't fault the computer's judgement.

When I finally stepped off the plane I was taken aback by the sheer blasting intensity of the heat. I had expected it to be a bit warm, of course, but nothing I had experienced in the Canaries could have prepared me for this. The airport policeman stamped a three month visa onto my passport without a murmur and I had a nosey around outside to find a cheap way of getting to the coast.

Most of the travellers were sharing taxis for about twenty quid between them but I discovered a local bus which did the same run for under thirty pence. Before long I had checked into a budget hotel and was able to enjoy a well-earned kip.

That evening, after I had phoned Jase and Scarlet, I decided to check out the local nightlife, so, scrubbed and changed, I made my way to the lobby. I was in the process of gleaning information about where to go from the hotel manager, when I overheard a bloke chatting on the phone in a familiar European accent. His name was Marco. He was Italian and had been travelling round South and Central America for ages. He was going out that night and agreed to show me the town.

We met up in the lobby again at about ten o'clock. We were both hungry so we decided to get something to eat at a nearby restaurant before hitting the clubs. He was a thoroughly pleasant bloke and and seemed very knowledgeable about the area so I took the opportunity to pick his brains about the possibility of getting a job in one of the nearby timeshare resorts. He warned me that it would be very difficult to get a work visa but that he had really no idea about the timeshare industry. We were having a good laugh and enjoying a few drinks when a faint warning bell began to sound in the back of my mind. Usually you can tell whether someone is gay just by talking to them, but what with the long journey and his being from a different country, I think I must have missed some of the usual tell-tale signs. I wasn't really sure, so I decided to find out.

'So, Marco, what's it like for girls around here then?' I asked pointedly, studying him intensely for a response.

'Hmmph,' he replied noncommittaly, pushing a chip round his plate with his fork.

'These Mexican birds are lovely, aren't they?' I persevered. 'Had a few have you?'

'I was wondering when this would happen,' he announced. 'I'm not exactly straight!'

'You mean you're gay?' I asked him. 'Well, that's no problem for me. Just don't let me catch you staring at my arse.'

I have never been particularly homophobic. All the same, in the light of this new information, I suddenly became acutely aware of my surroundings. We were sitting, just the two of us, at a candle-lit table by the restaurant window, overlooking the street. I cringed at the thought of people looking in and assuming that we were a couple – even the waiter seemed to be smirking, all things considered. I promptly changed my wine order for a pint of beer and struck up a loud conversation about fighting. By the end of the meal I was confident that my heterosexuality had been well and truly established but, just to be sure, I checked a few recent football scores with the waiter on the way out.

The clubs in town were wild and had a good mix of nationalities, so I didn't have to speak Spanish all night. I got home about ten o'clock the next morning – just in time to go and meet Scarlet at the airport. She was very excited and found it most amusing that I had made friends with Marco.

Scarlet and I spent the next few days traipsing round Cancun's timeshare resorts looking for a job. Marco's prediction about work permits proved correct and nobody wanted to employ us. We got completely demotivated by the constant rejection and at times, as we pounded the pavement in search of opportunity, the heat became almost unbearable. Walking down one particulary desolate-looking road, Scarlet drew my attention to a hand-painted sign urging us to beware of alligators. Thinking it to be a hoax, I jumped over the fence to investigate. To my horror, resting by the side of the water were five or six mud-coloured, triassic-looking predators. The glare from their emotionless eyes burnt into me as I silently climbed back over the fence and suggested that we 'fuck off, a bit lively'! There was no barrier to speak of and those beasts could have quite easily, should the mood have taken them, followed us up the road. Overhead, huge Andean albatrosses circled like pterodactyls, furthering the impression that we were stuck in some long-forgotten world.

Soon we had pretty much given up hope of finding employment. There was one last guy we had to meet and if he had nothing for us, we were just going to concentrate on enjoying ourselves for the remainder of our time in Mexico. We had arranged to go for a drink with him in a local nightclub. He was the marketing manager of a medium-sized resort and he had expressed an interest in having us setting up a photo team for him. The OPCs didn't use scratch cards out there and he thought that the photo programme would have a good chance of working.

When he turned up at the club, it soon emerged that all he was interested in was trying to get hold of Scarlet. She milked him for our drinks' bill, but we had to resign ourselves to the fact that we were obviously not destined to work in Mexico. That said, we all let our hair down for the rest of the night and had a bloody good time.

The next day I woke up mid-morning and was surprised to notice that Scarlet wasn't there – not that her staying out all night was out of the ordinary, but I thought she might have been a bit more cautious about going home with a stranger, given that we were in uncharted territory and a long way from home. I need not have worried. She turned up at teatime gushing with enthusiasm over a new place that she wanted us all to move in to. Isla Mujeres, it was called, and that was where she had spent the day. Taking her word for it, we packed up and left. Marco was now our pal and he came with us. As I said, he was a nice enough bloke, but when he and Scarlet got together they could really be too much. They would walk a small distance away, commenting on passing blokes, just loud enough for me to hear and get irritated by it. Every so often I would snap and shout, 'Enough already!' or some such thing, and then they would laugh at me, and I'd kick myself for taking the bait.

Scarlet hadn't exaggerated about the Isla Mujeres. Literally translated the name means Island of Women, referring to some ancient expeditionary force that discovered the place when all the local men were off fishing. Only the beautiful native women were left behind tending to the chores, leading the explorers to believe that this was some kind of lost tribe of goddesses who had somehow survived unmarred by the attentions of the coarser half of the species.

To get there we took the ferry at a cost of only eighty pence. It was about five miles across the Caribbean sea and, when we got there, I was totally knocked for six. The hotel cost four pounds a night, with swimming pool, air conditioning, electricity and hot water, and was right on the edge of *the* most heavenly beach I have ever seen or could ever have imagined. The sand was the colour and texture of flour and the beach was lined with the kind of palm trees whose trunks run parallel to the ground for most of their length before suddenly tilting and exploding into a firework display of green. The sea was light blue and as warm as the surrounding air. For the first couple of days on the island I just spent my time on the beach. Generally, I would sleep under a palm tree for most of the morning before making my way to one of the beach bars for a few games of chess with one of the locals. Happy hour was called at about four o'clock and all the American and European travellers would meet up to socialise over half-price marghuerita's. There were no seats at the beach bars, only swings suspended from the ceilings, and hammocks. From there we would carry on drinking into the evening against the backdrop of spectacular, haunting, Mexican sunsets.

After which, we would pop back to the hotel to shower and change before going out to a restaurant. A meal in the fanciest places around would only set you back around ninety pence, including drinks, dessert and coffee. From there it was a choice between a local bar or taking the ferry over to Cancun to party the night away on the busier clubs of the mainland. Either way, drinks were cheap. Whichever bar you went to would give you the option of paying for your drinks individually or investing seven pounds in a stamp on the back of your hand. The latter entitled you to as much alcohol as you could handle. I kid you not. For seven quid you could go to the bar as often as you wanted and order whatever drinks you liked.

Only an idiot could fail to have a good time in a paradise like this, you're probably thinking. But, in my defence, there were some contributory factors to my fall from grace.

One evening I was on the piss with a few of my new pals when I met an American girl who enticed me up to dance. We were smooching closely on the crowded floor when a Mexican bloke stumbled into me.

'Watch yourself there pal,' I warned, pleasantly enough, gently pushing him away. To my surprise, rather than apologising, the obnoxious so-and-so proceeded to dance right in front of me, flinging his arms in my face as if to suggest that I was in *his* space and had better move. Well, I was drunk anyway, having made more than my fair share of visits to the bar replete with free drinks stamp. Also, with the benefit of hindsight, I think much of the anger I never vented when I lost all that money in Coventry was still simmering below the surface, just waiting for an opportunity to come exploding out.

Anyway, leaving the psycho-babble aside for a moment, I'll tell you what happened. Common sense tells you not to get into trouble when you're so far from home, but when I looked at this arrogant sod, playing up in front of me, I just snapped. I belted him right on the nose and he went down like a sack of spuds. His mates tried to tear into me but Mexican blokes are only about 5ft tall and I kept knocking them down, one after the other. Again and again they came at me but I fought like a man possessed and was still going strong when the police arrived. Talk about a sobering experience. The Mexican Old Bill don't mess about, about ten of them turned up in a pick-up truck and I was scared to death. All the older coppers had white painted sub-machine-guns hanging round their necks and even the younger guys, some of whom couldn't have been more than 17, were brandishing pistols. They came running at me and I immediately threw my hands in the air, explaining that I didn't want any trouble.

'Neither do we!' growled one of them, as they manhandled me into the back of the truck. I was pinned face down on the floor with my arms held aloft and all their boots resting on my back. It was bloody uncomfortable and the journey took about half an hour. When we got to the medieval-looking police station I was frisked, all my possessions were tipped into a drawer and I was flung into a cell. A shaft of moonlight was shining through the barred, Dshaped window that opened to the street about 5ft above my head. It illuminated a dense cloud of mosquitoes and allowed me to see several giant cockroaches as they clicked their way confidently across the floor. The other, more sinister resident of the cell was an enormous spider in the far corner of the ceiling. I didn't even attempt to go to sleep in case it tried to sink its fangs into me. I needn't have worried. The last thing the police had planned for me was sleep. I had been in my cell for no more than fifteen minutes when the door clanged open. A drunken Mexican bloke was thrown in and the coppers told him in no uncertain terms that he was there to give me a kicking. In my heightened state of alertness, I was more than up to the challenge. I booted him round the cell and was repeatedly banging his head against the bars when the police finally dragged me off him and dumped him in another cell. Every time some new, Friday night brawler was arrested he was flung into my cell. Every time the result was the same – I think I was too terrified to act differently, and by the end of the night, the police appeared to have a grudging respect for me.

Not the commanding officer though. He amused himself during the night by trailing his truncheon along the bars of the cell doors and telling me that no-one knew where I was. I was likely, he told me, to be there for six months or so before going to trial. And, in his opinion, I would probably be sentenced to another six months in an even worse prison on the mainland. Stupid as it might sound but in the middle of the night in that God-forsaken jail, I believed every word. I was truly petrified, though I tried not to let it show just in case he was winding me up. When I asked about food and drink, I was told that no food was provided by them and that I would have to wait for my friends to bring me something to eat. In a panic I reminded them that no-one knew I was here, but this, they told me, was tough! I had a raging thirst too but again their response was minimal. One of them picked up a broken plastic cup from the floor and filled it up from the dirty old shower head at the end of the cell block. The cup was leaking from a slit down one side so there wasn't much time for indecision. Thanking God that I had had all my injections, I necked the lot.

It was another twenty-four hours until Scarlet managed to locate me. She hadn't been there when it all kicked off and was under the impression that I had sloped off with the American girl. When I hadn't come home the next day she had started to get worried and when she asked around, the other travellers had informed her of my arrest. She had checked every police station on the island before finally locating me. By that time I was suicidal and when I heard her voice at the main desk I was overcome with relief. She was allowed in briefly to see me, and I have to confess, I was in tears. Scarlet understood and stayed there as long as she was allowed to comfort me. Then she ran off to get me a food parcel. She spent the morning finding out what she had to do to get me out of there and managed to secure me a trial for the same day. Unwashed and stinking, I was led round to the courthouse to answer the charges and Scarlet was recorded as my official interpreter.

It turned out that the bar owner had called the police. The lads I was fighting with didn't even want to give evidence. Fair play to them. Whatever else they had done, they weren't grasses. No, what was going on was far more sinister. The bar owner, an unpleasant looking little bisexual fellow called Miguel, turned up dressed to the nines with a smart-looking lawyer in tow. He had filed the complaint with the intention of fleecing me, as I was soon to discover.

I sat in the dock trying to overhear the softly spoken Spanish conversation between the judge and the court reporter, but the heavy local dialect was confusing me. I didn't have long to wait and soon the charges against me were read out. As far as I could tell it was something to do with destruction of property. The judge told me that if I pleaded guilty I would be let off with a caution. Puzzled, I readily agreed. I seemed to be one step closer to freedom. Before I could saunter out of court however, the judge rapped her gavel and told me that we still had to sort out the matter of compensation. Perplexed, I sat back down and listened while Miguel asked for one thousand dollars to make up for all the damage I had inflicted on his bar. My mouth dropped open at that. I had broken nothing. And anyway, the bar was little more than a table from which beer was sold. The furniture was of the plastic garden variety and could not be broken without the use of some fairly heavy-duty cutting tools. In short, I could have destroyed the entire bar and still had change from a hundred bucks. Indignantly, I explained all this to the judge. She nodded understandingly and agreed that it did seem a bit excessive, but told me that if I contested the claim I would have to go back to prison for a couple of months while an independent investigation was carried out. Aha, I thought, now I understand. There was no way I was going back inside for another hour, let alone a couple of months. Miguel knew the system and had played it at my expense. I opted to cough up the dough and get out of there. Scarlet ran round collecting money off all the travellers we knew, with the promise that I would pay them back as soon as I got back to the hotel. I reckoned I could just about manage this, assuming Jason could lend me some money on arrival. I did just that and thanked Scarlet and everyone else profusely for their support. The nightmare seemed to be over and I hid in the hotel for some much-needed kip.

Jase was due to arrive at the airport later on that night so I got myself together and went off to meet him. He was so excited to be there that I didn't tell him about my escapades until we were on the bus. He was a bit subdued after hearing my story but we agreed not to let it spoil our remaining time in Mexico. It was another couple of hours before we got back to the Isla Mujeres and when we did, Scarlet was waiting for us. The judge from my trial had come looking for me while I was gone and there was yet more disturbing news. Miguel wasn't satisfied with the thousand bucks he had robbed from me and had made a further claim for two thousand dollars in lost business. It was ludicrous and the judge knew it but, as before, if I contested the claim I would have to languish in my cell for a couple of months while the investigation took place. The judge asked Scarlet to convey her advice to me, which was to do a runner further down the Quintana Roo in order to avoid being picked up by the local cozzers.

Poor old Jase. He had only just finished a twenty-hour journey and now, because of me, we had to set off again. With a deep sigh we shouldered our backpacks and headed off to the harbour.

It being the middle of the night, there were no ferries running. We bribed a fisherman who was just finishing work for the evening to take us over to the mainland. As luck would have it, a particularly nasty thunderstorm was raging. We clung onto our backpacks in the driving rain while lightning struck the sea all around us. We were extremely relieved when the lights of the shore drew close. The main harbour was shut so we had to settle for being dropped off on the beach.

After a couple of hours' walk, we finally found a road and started off in the direction of Cancun. A bus stopped for us and dropped us in the town centre. Miserable and cold, we flagged down a taxi to take us to a hotel. It really wasn't our night. All the hotels were full due to some national holiday and the cab driver was scaring us half to death by driving too fast and watching a portable television set while he was driving. We were about to give up hope when a hotel owner took pity on us and let us sleep on his living-room floor. We took a bus in the morning further down the coast to Playa del Carmen and settled there.

After we'd recovered from all the excitement, we managed to relax and enjoy our surroundings. We sunbathed, played chess and sampled the local nightlife. The one further event that imprinted itself on my memory was a snorkling trip that we stumbled upon, quite by accident.

It cost us seven quid each and lasted the whole day. We got to swim with dolphins, giant turtles, squids, octopii and even sharks. Due to the high oxygen content of the water, the nurse sharks were very docile. We could stroke them and even lift them out of the water for photos. That one-day trip may seem insignificant in the grand scale of things but for me it was what the whole thing was all about – travelling to the far corners of the earth to experience the wonders of nature is my main aim and ambition. I go through all the other motions because I have to, and because they provide me with the money to follow my dreams when I can.

Out of funds, I had to return to the UK after about eight weeks. In debt to my father, I had decided to get a regular job in an office until I could pay him back. It would be a struggle, conforming to the system, but I would face this challenge like any other and try not to let him down. This ahead of me, I leaned against the plane window as we jetted out of Cancun. As we rose higher I studied the intricate shadows that the setting sun was carving on the side of the thunder heads. Lightning was darting between the cloud banks as we flew by. I stretched back and closed my eyes, taking comfort from the wildness and beauty around me. With the impending necessity to get a 'proper' job and settle down in the UK, I had the strangest feeling that I was at the end of an era. I reflected on some of my adventures and some of the characters I had known. It had certainly been educating. Not to mention fun. And now it felt as though it was all over – it was finally time to grow up and start shouldering some responsibility, twenty-nine was too old to carry on acting like a teenager .

Then it struck me. Who said it was over? I had to pay Dad back the money I owed him, sure. But there was lots of travelling that I still wanted to do. It was only convention that was saying I had to settle down and I had spent the better part of my life so far defying convention. I had never been to Africa or Asia. I wanted to witness the Northern Lights from the frozen regions of Scandinavia and sky dive off Angel Falls. I wanted to navigate the Congo by boat and walk to Base Camp, Everest. I decided there and then to give myself the time to do these things. If you believe that you only have one life then why waste the first sixty-five years saving up for the last ten?

It occurred to me that for all the modern inventions and talk of the world getting smaller, it was still huge. You could live for a thousand years travelling from place to place and still only experience a fraction of what was on offer. The world had plenty left to see and it would all still be there when I had done my time in the UK. It was going to be a tough time ahead, getting a decent job and building a life that I had no intention of prolonging any longer than it took to pay off my debt, but with this goal in sight I knew that I would manage.

The 747 hurtled through the night towards Heathrow and I sank further back into my seat with a contented smile. It wasn't the end of an era: an era is a long, long time.